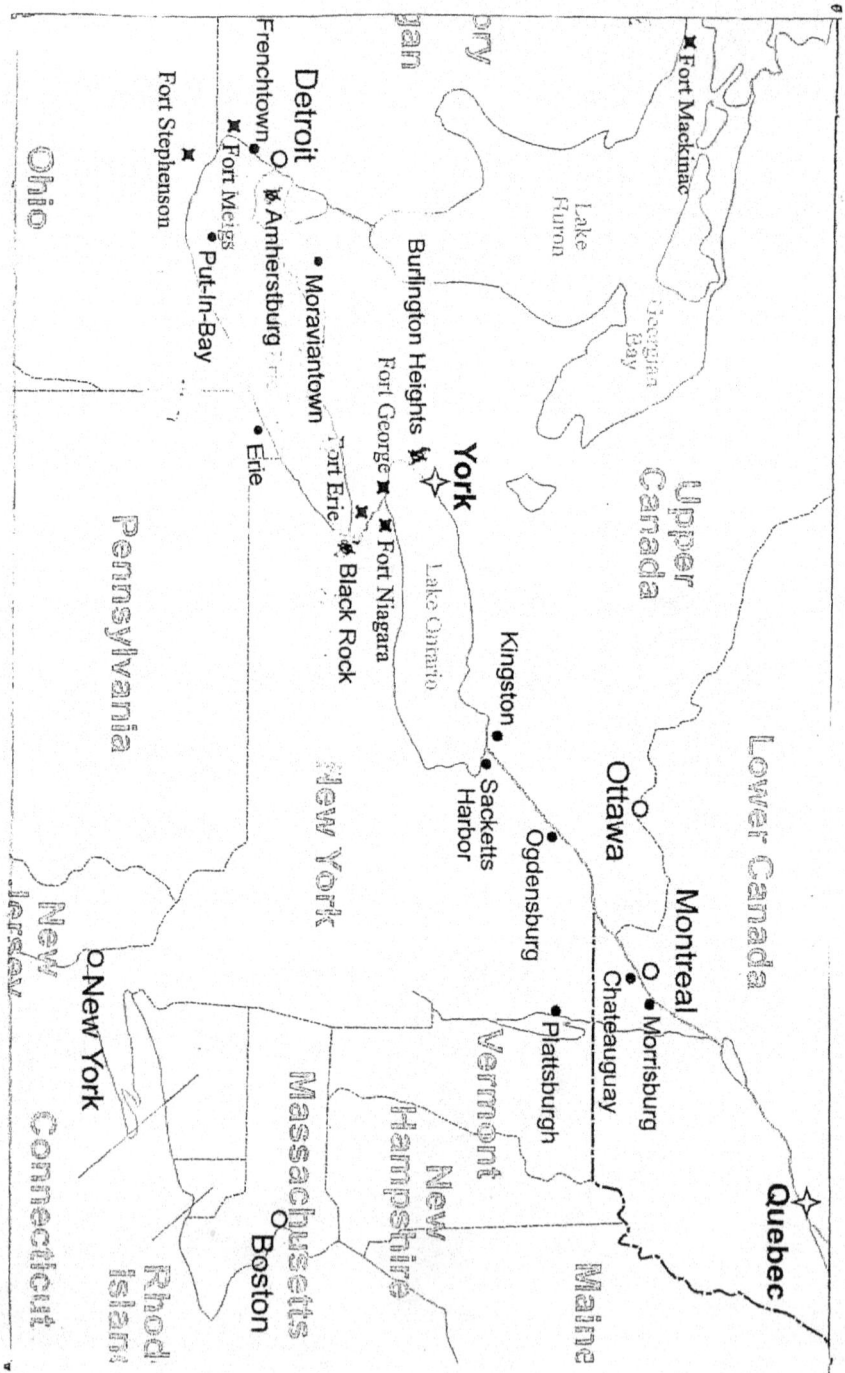

THREE STRIKES IN THE WAR OF 1812

THREE AMERICAN VICTORIES IN THE WAR OF 1812 THAT PERMANENTLY EJECTED THE BRITISH AND ULTIMATELY THEIR INDIAN ALLIES FROM WHAT IS NOW THE MIDWESTERN UNITED STATES EAST OF THE MISSISSIPPI

BY

William R. Miller

HERITAGE BOOKS
2016

HERITAGE BOOKS

AN IMPRINT OF HERITAGE BOOKS, INC.

Books, CDs, and more—Worldwide

For our listing of thousands of titles see our website
at
www.HeritageBooks.com

Published 2016 by
HERITAGE BOOKS, INC.
Publishing Division
5810 Ruatan Street
Berwyn Heights, Md. 20740

Copyright © 2016 William R. Miller

International Standard Book Numbers
Paperbound: 978-0-7884-5737-1
Clothbound: 978-0-7884-5973-3

Dedication

This book is dedicated first and foremost to my wife who patiently endured and also encouraged me as I struggled with this book and became increasingly oblivious to my surroundings, time and my other responsibilities.

I also must recognize all the great historians of the War of 1812, particularly those listed in the Bibliography, whose research provided me with most of the background information vital for my analysis.

Finally, I would like to express my appreciation for all the work that the very skilled and very patient editor at Heritage Books, Debbie Riley, did to make this book possible.

All proceeds from the sales of this book will go to support the Erie Maritime Museum.

Cover map from *A Country by Consent (www.canadianhistoryproject.ca/1774)*

Table of Contents

List of Illustrations

x

INTRODUCTION

"When you rise in the morning, give thanks for the light, for your life, for your strength. Give thanks for your food and for the joy of living. If you see no reason to give thanks, the fault lies in yourself."

Tecumseh

I have been an avid reader of history for all my life, but I am not a historian by education or career experience. Rather, I have been in management for over 50 years, 17 of which years I served as a corporate officer at major corporations. Challenging assignments in my career often involved analyzing all the similar aspects of business organization and operation.

A number of years ago, I became a Docent at the Erie Maritime Museum, which focuses on the Battle of Lake Erie. It was there that I became fascinated by the War of 1812 in particular. This book is my resultant attempt to apply analytical skills to shed new light on and offer insights into what transpired in three critical, interrelated victories in that War and the consequences thereof. It is my hope and belief that, by using an analytic approach and focusing on the Three Strikes that form the core of this book, I can offer the reader somewhat of a new perspective.

As a result, this is not a "reference type" history book, which would tend to have 100 pages or so of "Notes" at the end to permit other historians (professional and amateur) to trace the source of every fact or opinion contained. There are a number of excellent "reference type" history books on the War of 1812.[1]

This book instead aims to be an "analytic type" history book, which focuses first on an interrelated series of historical events and then analyses such concepts as causes, judgment, environment, consequences, etc. that come into play.

---

[1] *Such as Donald Hickey's well documented *The War of 1812*

Too often the War of 1812 is dismissed as a tie and therefore of little interest. That is too bad because it was actually one of the boldest gambles in the existence of the United States.

Because many segments of the nation had become infuriated and adversely affected by actions of the British Crown, Congress and President Madison declared war. However, from the onset, there were some other segments of the nation that did not favor the war and supported it only lukewarmly.

America had lots to lose in this gamble. Britain had made it plain, starting even before the Quebec Act of 1774, that its long range plan for North America was for the territory between the Appalachian Mountains and the Mississippi River to be partially part of Quebec and partially an Indian Homeland (buffer state). True to this thinking, one British demand at the opening of the Peace Treaty negotiations was to have America cede portions of the "old northwest": what would be Michigan, Wisconsin, Illinois, 80% of Indiana and 33% of Ohio.

To appreciate how gutsy America's move this was, one has only to look at the numbers. At the outbreak of war, it's army was outnumbered in manpower about 20 to 1 (229,000:11,750) and the navy outnumbered in warships 37 to 1 (740:20). In addition, the British could also draw on about 5,000 Indian fighters it had secured though treaties, compared to perhaps 500 from tribes who sided with the Americans.

The America government's assumption, that the Canadians would welcome them as liberators, also turned out to be bad. Most of the Canadian militia (about 10,000 strong) sided with England.

America also assumed that the British were so tied up in the Napoleonic War that they would have little in the way of regular troops to spare. This later hope was undermined by at least two factors. First, in return for promises of land they intended to acquire from America and turn into a homeland for the Indians, the British got thousands of Indian fighters to supplement their regulars. Second, in the middle of the War of 1812, Napoleon was defeated and abdicated. This freed up thousands of Redcoats, many of whom were battle hardened veterans.

It is my contention that the principal factors that prevented all of these above problems from turning into the total disaster for the United States, that one might expect from them (including massive lose of territory), were the Three Strikes. These three, interconnected victories prevented the British from being able to use the new reinforcements to mount any attacks anywhere west of Montreal. These three, interconnected victories forced the British to abandon their military presence west of the Appalachian Mountains and south of the Great Lakes. These three, interconnected victories led to the death of the key Indian leader, Tecumseh, the breakup of the Indian Confederacy and the loss of his thousands of warriors as allies.

Britain's resultant exclusion from the Great Lakes led their greatest military hero, Lord Wellington, to recommend to the negotiators meeting with the Americans to make peace without any territorial demands.

This book is the story about these Three Strikes. It starts with a Prequel Portrait Gallery that attempts to put a human face on key players in the three actions by providing a picture and a little bio about them. After briefly reviewing the causes and assumptions surrounding the declaration of war, there is a Chapter (Food, Guns and Germs) covering the environment in which the Three Strikes took place. Since each of the Strike actions themselves have been independently extensively analyzed in a number of history books such as those in the bibliography, the core chapter, on the Three Strikes, goes into additional detail principally about underreported aspects.

I realized after the book was mostly written, that there was a fourth factor that I had overlooked. In my defense, it was the "Great Battle of Lake Ontario," a battle which never actually took place. Nonetheless, it had a major impact on the Three Strikes.

Commander Yeo, the overall commander of the Royal Navy in the Canadian theatre siphoned off precious resources to staff and equip the Lake Ontario fleet for a confrontation with the American Lake Ontario fleet that never happened. There was little left to send on to help Commander Barclay on Lake Erie.

Luck played such a significant role in America being able to pull off this amazing string of victories, that I have devoted an entire Chapter to the Luck factor. The book then moves into the Peace Negotiation and the impact of the Three Strikes on them. The main book then winds up with post war actual events along with conjecture on outcomes had the Three Strikes failed. It also gets into the longer-range strategic consequences of the conflict.

Appendix - Finally, there was a lot of additional specific detail about many of the subjects covered in the book that were peripheral to the main theme. For those readers who would be interested, I have included these details into a series of Appendices to which readers can refer for more information on a particular subject.

Prequel - A Picture Gallery of the Principal Players in the Three Strikes and Subsequent Peace Conference

In order to put a more human face to the principal players involved in the Three Strikes and subsequent Peace Conference, included are portraits and a small write-up of each of them

Strike One

The American commander in charge of the Raid on York was General Henry Dearborn, who had also done the planning. At the time, he was 62 and so racked with rheumatism that he had to direct the action from his flagship anchored off shore. He delegated General Zebulon Pike to go in with the troops and be the on-site commander. Pike was killed when the British blew up the Armory. When it was over, Dearborn went ashore to sign the surrender documents. Despite having fought in many of the battles of the Revolutionary War, from Bunker Hill to Yorktown, Dearborn was considered at best a mediocre commander of troops.

The British commander at the defense of York was accidently thrust into the role. General Roger Sheaffe happened to be traveling through York with four companies of regulars, who were being sent to reinforce some western forts, when the Americans struck.

General Sheaffe had an interesting background. He was born in Boston in 1763 and attended Boston Latin School. One of his sisters married Robert Livingston, a signer of the Declaration of Independence. His family fell on hard times (perhaps related to their Loyalist leanings) but, fortunately for young Roger, Lord Percy took an interest in him and got him started on his military career. As an officer he gained a reputation for handing out harsh punishments even for minor transgressions. This culminated, when he was at Fort George, with the regular troops under his command mutinying. General Brock himself had to come and intervene.

Strike One

General Henry Dearborn, Commander of American forces at the Raid on the British Naval Base at York (present day Toronto)

Strike One

General Roger Hale Sheaffe, Commander of the British forces defending their Naval Base at York (present day Toronto)

Strike Two

The American commander at the Battle of Lake Erie was Commodore Oliver Hazard Perry. Only 28 at the time of the battle, he already had been in the Navy for 15 years, during which time he had been in a number of naval battles against pirates both on the Barbary Coast and the Caribbean. Perry came from a naval family. His father was a ship Captain in the Navy and his younger brother later became a Commodore himself. His cousin, Stephen Champlin, commanded the schooner *Scorpion* in Perry's squadron. Perry's mother was a descendant of William Wallace, the famous Scottish patriot (but a rebel in the eyes of the English).

The British Commander at the Battle of Lake Erie was Robert Barclay. Though he was one year younger still than Perry, he actually had spent more time at sea, having joined the navy at 11 years of age. Like Perry, by then he already had been in several naval battles, the most notable of which being Trafalgar. He had later lost his left arm leading a boarding party against the French.

The actions of Surgeon's Mate Usher Parsons, a medical hero of the Battle of Lake Erie, are discussed elsewhere in the text and in Appendix F.

Strike Two
Commodore Oliver Hazard Perry, commander of the
American fleet at the Battle of Lake Erie

Strike Two

Commander Robert Barclay, RN, commander of the British
fleet at the Battle of Lake Erie

Strike Two

Surgeon's Mate Usher Parsons - With both of the *Lawrence's* doctors too sick to serve, Parsons performed the surgeries during, and on the morning after, the battle.

Commodore James Lucas Yeo, Commander of all the Naval Ships on the Great Lakes (with his primary focus Lake Ontario). Commander Barclay on Lake Erie reported to him.

Strike Three

The American Commander at the Battle of the Thames (aka the Battle of Moraviantown) was General William H. Harrison. Born in 1773 in the Virginia Colony, he became the last US President elected who was born before the Revolution. His father was a signer of the Declaration of Independence. During the Indian Wars Harrison served under General "Mad Anthony" Wayne and led the successful attack on Tippecanoe (Prophetstown), Tecumseh's main base. (At the time, Tecumseh himself, with many of his warriors, was away negotiating with the southern Indian tribes). Harrison and Perry worked very well together in driving the British from the Old Northwest.

The English Commander at the Battle of Moraviantown was 50-year-old General Henry Procter. Prior to his commands in the War of 1812 he had had no combat experience. His mixed military record of successes and failures, culminating in his disastrous defeat at Moraviantown, earned him a place among the worst British commanders in the War of 1812.

Chief Tecumseh of the Shawnee, leader of the entire Indian Confederation and acting leader of the Indian warriors gathered at Ft. Amherstburg, is dealt with in some detail in the text and Appendix D and E of this book.

Strike Three
General William H. Harrison. commander of the
American Army at the Battle of Moraviantown

Artwork by C. H. J. Forster.   Public Domain

Strike Three
General Henry Procter, commander of the British forces
at the Battle of Moraviantown

Strike Three

Tecumseh, A Chief of the Shawnee who, with his brother Tenskwatawa (The Prophet) put together the America's last Indian Confederation and signed a Treaty with the Crown. He was killed at the Battle of Moraviantown. (Note the Medal from King George in the painting)

Peace Negotiations at Ghent, Belgium

Chief American Peace Conference Negotiator John Quincy Adams was born in 1767. Like Harrison, his father was a signer of the Declaration of Independence. In the early days of the nation, his father served as US Ambassador to a number of nations. John Quincy traveled with his dad; he learned about the countries and spoke several languages. At the time the War of 1812 broke out, he himself was serving as Ambassador to Russia.

John Quincy Adam's strong, Number Two, negotiator was Henry Clay, Speaker of the House. Clay, in his long political career, showed himself to be one of the greatest negotiators and compromise brokers in the history of the US.

With John Quincy Adams and Henry Clay, backed up by Secretary of the Treasury Albert Gallatin, Jonathan Russell (the President's representative in Paris) and James A. Bayard (a leading member of the opposition party, the Federalists), America had sent it's "A Team" to the Peace Conference.

Normally, one might have expected to see the British send their Foreign Secretary Lord Castlereagh and Secretary for War and the Colonies Lord Bathurst to the Peace Conference. These, however, were not "normal" times. Napoleon had surrendered and abdicated and the top diplomats of Britain, Prussia, Austria, Russia and France were gathered at the Congress of Vienna to try to work out a lasting peace and, in the process, redraw the map of Europe. In addition to these major powers, close to 100 other political entities also were represented at the Congress. As a result, Britain's top diplomats were tied up in Vienna. The Ghent meeting got the "B" team, although Castlereagh would stop by on his way to and from Vienna to give (and revise) guidelines.

The Lead Negotiator on site in Ghent was Admiral Baron James Gambier. Born in 1756, he had a long, active and distinguished career in the Navy. The only cloud was his 1809

Court Martial for not following up after he had succeeded in driving a French fleet aground by using explosion vessels. He was exonerated (and his accusers never got another command).

It may come as a surprise that Kenyon College, in present day Gambier, Ohio and considered by some as one of the "Little Ivies" was founded in 1824 to a large extent by a major donation from Admiral Gambier. The Admiral was a devout Anglican and the college was originally established partially for the education of Episcopal priests.

19th Century engraving from portrait by George Peter Alexander Healy
Library of Congress   Public Domain

Peace Negotiations at Ghent, Belgium
John Quincy Adams, Lead Negotiator of the American Team for
the War of 1812 Peace Treaty

Peace Negotiations at Ghent, Belgium
Henry Clay, Speaker of the House and Number Two Negotiator
on the American Team for the War of 1812 Peace Treaty

Peace Negotiations at Ghent, Belgium

Robert Stewart, 2nd Marquees of Londonderry; Lord Castlereagh.- Foreign Secretary and Leader of the House of Commons. (Since he was tied up at the Vienna Congress, he appointed Admiral Gambier to lead the negotiations with the United States, but he stopped in regularly to provide guidance).

Peace Negotiations at Ghent, Belgium
Admiral Baron James Gambier, Lead Negotiator of the British
Team for the War of 1812 Peace Treaty

Arthur Wellesley, 1st Duke of Wellington – Commander of the Anglo-Allied Army in the Waterloo Campaign. Most famous and most decorated British General of the early 1800s. Wellington provided the professional assessment of the British situation in the War of 1812 that led the negotiators to signing the Peace Treaty.

Chapter I - The Three Primary Reasons that the US Declared War on Britain

"You must bear in mind that these strangers are not as you – they are devoid of natural affection, loving gold and gain better than one another or their own souls"

Tecumseh

A - Blockade

Both England and France endeavored to prevent the US from supplying food to the other. However, since England's warships dominated the high seas and the much smaller French fleet rarely ventured out, in practice it was the British who blocked American trade. American ships either had to trade with England or, if they wanted to go to a port on the Continent, stop in England first to pay tariff and get permission. This put a serious dent in America's burgeoning trade and made American merchants very vocal in their pleas to Congress for redress.

B - Impressment of Sailors on US Merchant Ships into the Royal Navy

1. Impressment – The "Why" of it

Estimates of Manpower Available for Army and Navy

Great Britain in 1800 was a relatively small nation, in population, attempting to compete militarily with the far larger, more heavily-populated nations of the European mainland. With such a high percent of the male population needed to staff the military and be away from home for many years, the birth rate somewhat depressed..

1801 Census Data

Population - England & Wales	8.9 million
Population – Scotland	1.6 million
Population – Ireland (est.)	<u>5 million</u>
TOTAL	15.5 million

Percent of population 15 or younger – 36%
Percent of population over 65 – 4%
Assumed percent female - 50%
Percent of militarily eligible males –
    $(100\% - 36\% - 4\%) \times 0.5 = 30\%$
Gross manpower pool $15.5 \times 0.3 = 4.55$ million

Further Adjustments

Since Ireland and Scotland were historically subject to frequent uprisings, the actual available manpower for service in the British armed forces, from these areas, may be overstated. For instance, there was a major rebellion in Ireland in 1798 and, after years of unrest, the Scots rose again in 1820. These rebellions tied up some of the Army and made recruitment difficult.

A higher percentage of these individuals at the upper end of the age range would have been in poorer health compared to that same group today. Therefore, availability of able-bodied men in the 45 to 65 age range is probably overstated.

In 1801 England, 37% of the males in the pool were needed just to grow the food to feed the country's population. This adjustment alone cuts the available pool to 2.9 million

With all these adjustments, the realistic available manpower pool was probably closer to 2 million. Even taking from this pool ran the danger of siphoning off critically-needed skilled labor in the burgeoning Industrial Revolution, particularly in mining and the textile trades.

Military Manpower needs:

1812 British Army 229,000
1812 British Navy 145,000 (to man 740 ships)
1812 British Homeland Militia 121,000
TOTAL 495,000 (½ a million men; 25% of the pool!)

Both army and navy had battle casualties to replace but the navy had a unique and larger cause of manpower shortage. As is cited elsewhere in this book, poor shipboard hygiene and the difficulty in keeping food from spoiling on long voyages meant that sickness was a more constant and severe drain on the seamen ranks than the infrequent naval engagements. (See Chapter III.C.1)

2. The Impressment Solution

With a dangerously high percent of the "available" home- country males already in the armed services, with limited capability to teach seamanship (and gunnery) and with the need for crewman who could understand commands in English from the officers, impressment of sailors from American merchant ships seemed like an ideal solution to the English warship captains.

Initially the British claimed they were just looking for and seizing English Navy deserters who had jumped ship for the better pay and working conditions of the US merchantmen. As the war with France rolled on, year after year, the English ship captains increasingly became less and less scrupulous about whether the sailor was an American citizen.

C. Britain in a "Guns for Furs" Trade Armed the Indians that were Harassing the Settlers

Great Britain had a very lucrative fur trade going with the Indian tribes west of the mountains. In order to service and protect this trade, they maintained forts and fortified trading posts in Canada and some of the disputed territory from the Mississippi River to the Appalachian Mountains.

It also was to England's strategic benefit if the tide of settlers streaming west could be checked. Western Canada was virtually unsettled and access to that region by traveling from or through the US was far easier than the route through Canada north of the Great Lakes.. The English were concerned about the potential "Americanization" of Western Canada before the area could be "Canadianized". Forming treaties and alliances with the various mid western Indian Tribes therefore made good sense to British interests in many ways.

The now well-armed Indians with their food supplies more assured (*See* Food – Indian Availability) were able to mount serious attacks on settlers encroaching on land the Indians considered theirs (historically and/or by way of a treaty). The very small American Regular Army couldn't offer much help and the settlers were very vocal in their complaints to Congress about Britain's hand in the Indian raids.

Chapter II - The Three Bad Assumptions that Congress and President Madison Made In Declaring War on England

"A single twig breaks, but the bundle of sticks is strong"
and
"The only way to fight this evil is for the red man to unite in claiming a common and equal right to the land, as it was first, and should be now, for it was never divided"
and
"Let us form one body, one heart, and defend to the last warrior our country, our homes, our liberty, and the graves of our fathers"
Tecumseh

A. Assumption about England's involvement and Commitment to the War in Europe

The American politicians assumed that, with virtually all their Army tied up fighting Napoleon, the British would not be able to commit sufficient forces to fighting in America and would instead sue for a negotiated settlement of the American grievances. As a corollary, Congress assumed that France would be able to help the American cause again as they had during the Revolution. ("The enemy of my enemy is my friend" theory). In particular, they assumed the French Fleet would help level the playing field at sea, where the British Navy outnumbered the American Navy by something like 740 to 17 vessels,

B. Assumption about the Canadians' reception of Americans

The American politicians assumed that the Canadians would welcome the Americans as "liberators" come to free them from the British oppressors. They even envisioned Canadian militia fighting alongside them against the British occupiers.

Although the cross-border relations had been fairly good in the period between the wars, the Americans underestimated the strong "Loyalist" factor in the Canadian population. Many of the Canadians of 1812 were in fact former residents of the original American colonies who had remained loyal to England during the Revolution and had fled to Canada to escape the inevitable persecution when the colonies achieved their independence. It also turned out that French-speaking Canadians, in general, distrusted the Americans even more than they distrusted the British.

Many Canadians therefore considered the US incursions into Canada as an act of invasion rather than liberation. Most of the Canadian militia remained loyal to the Crown and fought alongside the British regulars opposing the Americans.

C. Assumption about the Indians

The American politicians assumed that the Indians were ignorant savages continually fighting among themselves and incapable of concerted action. They didn't take the Indians into consideration as they weighed the pros and cons of going to war with England.

They never considered the possibility that an Indian leader (or leaders) could arise who could unify a significant portion of the Indian Nations and tribes into a political and military entity. The Shawnee chief Tecumseh (See Appendix D) and his brother Tenskwatawa (aka the Prophet) were able to seize leadership in a spontaneous Indian religious revival and use it to build Confederation of Six Major tribes (which also attracted a significant number of warriors from other tribes).

The Americans, as a result, never anticipated that the Indian tribes would be able to provide the British with large numbers of trained and equipped fighters to supplement the limited numbers of regulars that could be spared from the fighting on the Continent. Until the death of Tecumseh (Strike Three) the

Indians provided thousands of fighters to supplement the regulars and militia, greatly enhancing the British military capability.

Robert Dickson, a long term, very successful fur trader in the western part of the Old Northwest, also was able to put together another group of tribes from his area. In order to obtain their support, he apparently made many promises on behalf of the Crown, including support on their land claims. Dickson was somewhat unusual in that he lived most of his life among the Indians and even had a wife who was a Sioux. At least initially, he had as many or possibly more warriors to call upon than Tecumseh.

Fortunately for the Americans, unlike Tecumseh's tribes, Dickson's tribes had no religious crusade further binding them together. They were in it primarily for plunder rather than promises of land in the future. The coordinated Indian-British attacks against the American forts and forces in Ohio in late 1812 and early 1813 largely met with failure. Dickson's Indian allies therefore began returning to their villages and had largely vanished from the field by the Battle of Moraviantown.

Chapter III – Food, Guns and Germs

"I told the boys to go ... but the boys won't go."
Erie Militia Captain to Perry about manning the shore batteries

"It is very obvious to me that you must remove Sir George Prevost. I see he has gone to war about trifles with the general officers I sent him, which are certainly the best of their rank in the army; and his subsequent failure and distresses will be aggravated by that circumstance; and will probably with the usual fairness of the public be attributed to it."
Duke of Wellington

"Live your life that the fear of death can never enter your heart"
Tecumseh

Jared Diamond, in his landmark book *Guns, Germs, and Steel* utilizes groupings of certain historical factors. Similar factors also were very much in play in the Three Strikes. Diamond also points out the importance of advances in agriculture, which made it possible for only a fraction of a given society's population to produce the food for the entire population. This freed up people for the trades, making products that benefited all. It freed up men to man the armies and navies which enabled extended warfare.

A – Food

1. Problem with Colonial Era Militias

In the 1800 Census, it was determined that 83% of the workforce in the US (and probably even a higher percentage in Canada) was involved in agriculture. Looking at it another way, five of every six workers were engaged in growing and processing food. This meant that any sizable US and Canadian militia force could not be spared for very long or everyone at home would starve. Time and again, in the various campaigns reliant on the availability of militia, the victorious force couldn't follow up on the victory because the militia would not serve far from home and, when needed on the farm, simply went home.

2. Impact of Indian Fighters' Availability

Native American agriculture had developed slowly as an adjunct and alternative to their traditional hunter-gatherer lifestyle. Growth in Indian agriculture before the arrival of the settlers was hampered by the fact that there were no indigenous, suitably large, animals in all of North America that could be domesticated. Human labor was inefficient except for small plots.

The crops that were raised were a somewhat different mix than that to which the settlers were accustomed. The Iroquois appear to have coined the name "Three Sisters" for the three synergistic crops the Indians grew together on the same plot.

Sister Bean (Modern agricultural science now realizes that the bean plant fixed, or made available in plant form, nitrogen from the air).
Sister Corn (As a side benefit, this plant provided the support for Sister Bean's trailing vine).
Sister Squash (The squash plant, as a side benefit, provided ground cover to hold moisture and maintain a healthy soil environment as well as deterring animal invaders with its spiny stems.

In the past, between hunter-gatherer efforts and what were little more than vegetable gardens, it took the whole population to supply the food needed for the tribe. One consequence was that intertribal warfare consisted largely of short raids since the warriors could not be spared for long periods. When the settlers arrived, bringing with them horses, oxen and cattle, Native American agriculture embarked on a "mini-green revolution" in the fertile plains west of the mountains stretching to the Mississippi Valley and beyond.

Without this transition to animal-powered farming, where less manpower was required to raise the food, Tecumseh never could have brought thousands of warriors to fight in extended campaigns sometimes hundreds of miles from their homes. This change was underappreciated by Congress in their war planning, It was a major factor in allowing the British, with only about 10,000 less experienced[1] Redcoats and 12,000 short-enlistments, territorially limited, Canadian militia available, to blunt repeated A.merican attempts to invade Canada or even launch raids on the U.S.

3. The British Situation at Amherstburg

In 1812, the area around Detroit and Amherstburg, across the river, was sparsely settled. The local farmers could not produce anywhere near the amount of food necessary to feed the number of people stationed at the local forts. There were almost 1,000 regulars, a similar number of sailors and shipwrights and the Indian allies, some of whom, to make matters worse, had brought their families with them. Some estimates put the number of Indians that had to be fed at Amherstburg alone as high as 14,000. In the earlier series of battles between British forces and American forces for control of this area, both sides had "requisitioned" food from local farms to feed their troops. This had depleted what stores there were available in the region.

Before the advent of Perry's control of eastern Lake Erie, supplies could be and were brought down by ship from the more abundant farms on Canada's Niagara Peninsula. Perry cut this

---

[1]The best trained, battle-tested British troops were committed to the war with Napoleon. The troops sent to fight in Canada for the most part were less well-trained and equipped.

supply line. From the top of the Portage Escarpment, which runs parallel to the shore of Lake Erie in upper New York State and Pennsylvania,, it is possible to see all the way to Long Point, Canada with the naked eye. Any British ships that tried to sneak supplies up Lake Erie to Amherstburg would be spotted.

General Procter, the British commandant at Amherstburg had no recourse but to put all the British regulars and seamen on half rations. He urgently pressured Barclay, who was commanding the British squadron assembled at Amherstburg, to destroy Perry's blockading fleet and reopen the supply lines.

Procter's only other alternative would be to abandon the forts and fall back to the British bases on western Lake Ontario. This second alternative was made all the more undesirable by the fact that it might be viewed as a retreat and/or a sign of weakness by his Indian Allies. Worse still, Tecumseh himself, the leader of the Indian Confederation, was at Amherstburg at the time, along with 1,000 of his warriors. Tecumseh was opposed to any talk of retreat. (*See* Tecumseh's letter in Appendix E). Commander Barclay, his fleet staffed with half-starved, inexperienced seamen and with his flagship outfitted with a mixed bag of artillery, was ordered to sally out to attack the American fleet.

4. Food and the Battle of the Thames

After the Battle of Lake Erie, the American fleet, now numbering 15 vessels, was in complete control of all ship movement on Lake Erie and there was no hope of food resupply to the forts. General Procter was forced to destroy the forts at Detroit and Amherstburg and began his retreat headed east up the Thames River.[2] Procter had available about 800 (half-starved) regulars, as well as Tecumseh with 500 of his warriors. Since most of the cannon had been used to arm the fleet, the British had few cannon.

---

[2] The Thames runs roughly parallel to the north shore of Lake Erie.

Perry's ships had ferried most of General Harrison's (well fed) army of 3,800, only 120 of which were American regulars, across Lake Erie. Harrison's biggest edge was his 1,000 volunteer cavalrymen and he also had 250 Indian allies with him. As Harrison pursued Procter, three of Perry's shallowest draft ships sailed as far up the Thames as they could go in support of Harrison. Other of Perry's ships kept pace, sailing along the north shore of Lake Erie with reserve supplies. With this kind of logistical support Harrison's horses were probably better fed than Procter's men. (Perry himself turned the command of the fleet over to Eliot and rode with General Harrison).

Starvation no doubt contributed to the surrender by most of the British regulars after only one volley. With the full force of Harrison's army now brought to bear on them, the equally hungry Indians scattered and were unable to prevent the loss of their leader, Tecumseh. As said elsewhere, with him died the Confederation and the hope of an Indian homeland.

B - Guns

1. In Strikes One and Two

As described in the Strike One chapter, twenty of the 24- pounder carronades destined for the newly-built *Detroit* waiting in Amherstburg, along with the vital gunlock firing mechanisms for the these cannon, had been captured by American raiders at York and could not be replaced in time. That meant that the *Detroit* had to be equipped with a mismatched assortment of, "fortress type" long guns. (Each of these long guns required a twelve man crew and had a slower firing rate than similar caliber carronades). Many matches and linstocks that the British had on hand, turned out to be defective. The *Detroit* was reduced to having to fire its cannons by discharging flintlock pistols over the primer holes.

The result of all this was that the 18 very large caliber and fast-firing 32 pounder carronades, with which both the *Lawrence* and the *Niagara* were equipped could deliver more pounds per minute of cannon balls than the *Detroit* with its mix of guns.

The American fleet had a significant edge in addition to just the speed of fire. It also had a significant edge in total pounds of metal per broadside. The American squadron's guns could deliver a total of 896 pound of metal compared to 459 pounds from all the British cannon. (See Appendix A - "Cannon Facts)

2. The Situation Aloft

Traditionally, in naval battles of the period, Marine sharpshooters would be positioned up in the ships' rigging targeting the officers, sailors and gun crews of the opposing vessel. As noted elsewhere, Commander Yeo on Lake Ontario (Barclay's superior) couldn't spare Royal Marines so Barclay had to utilize soldiers of the 41st Foot Regiment for this role. Perry, had no Marines either and used Kentucky and Ohio militiamen instead.

There were at least two important differences between fleets. The first is armament. The Redcoats were armed with muskets. In massed volley fire, muskets were effective to 100 yards but for individual firing at targets they really were only effective for perhaps 50 yards. Furthermore, the British were used to firing and reloading on solid ground. Many of the American frontiersmen carried their own long rifles which, in the hands of an experienced marksman, could hit the target at 200 yards.

The second difference was that the British armed forces were structured much more hieratically. The Americans quickly learned the advantage of taking out the officers. It is probably no accident that every senior officer on the *Detroit* and the *Queen Charlotte* was either killed or wounded. (American fighters were more independent in action so loss of an officer was somewhat less critical).

C- Germs

1. The American Situation

Presqu' Isle Bay, where Perry was building his fleet, was stagnant in many areas. The few streams flowing in to flush it out were low flow waterways, particularly during the summer.

Erie was a small settlement of roughly 500 souls and the sudden and substantial influx of shipbuilders and seamen overwhelmed the primitive sanitary facilities. The situation was not helped by the normal practice among sailing ships at the time, which was simply to throw trash, including human waste, overboard. This might not pose a problem for ships underway or anchored in flowing water. With boats anchored for long periods of time in still waters, however, it was a ticking time bomb.

Since it is shallow, Presqu' Isle Bay also gets fairly warm in summer and this encourages germ growth. Dysentery therefore became rampant among the sailors, soldiers and shipbuilders.

Epidemics of dysentery were frequent occurrences aboard sailing vessels, as well as in army camps, and other places where large groups of human beings lived together in close quarters with poor sanitation. The Royal Navy lost 103,660 men fighting the French between 1793 and 1815. Of these, only 6,540 (6.3%) were killed in action. Most of the rest died from disease.

2. Battle of Lake Erie (Battle between the Starving and the Sick)

The "Food" and "Germs" factors discussed here certainly affected the outcome of the Battle and, therefore, history. Both sides went into battle with severe impediments to their fighting ability. Perry himself was so sick with the disease that he had to take to his bed the day before the battle. Aboard the heavily-engaged *Lawrence*, the senior ship doctors were too weak to perform their duties so a

Surgeon's Mate, Usher Parsons, became the only functioning (acting) doctor. An examination of the medical records of Perry's fleet showed that, out of a total complement of 532, only 416 (78%), were fit for duty on the day of the Battle. About one quarter of the crews on both the *Lawrence* and the *Niagara* were unfit for duty on the day of the battle.

Perry's men, however, did benefit from their pre-battle sojourn in Put-in-Bay on South Bass Island in western Lake Erie; away from the pollution they had helped cause in Erie, and with the fresh spring water in the caves near the anchorage. Barclay's men, who had been on half rations for weeks, got no relief from their food (and grog) shortage.

3. The Accidental Pioneer of Sterilization

Quite a different battle was being fought in the wardrooms below decks on every ship.[3] The "battle" taking place in surgeries was between possibly fatal organisms and the surgeons, who were trying to save the patients' lives.

Aboard the *Lawrence,* the two regular surgeons were so sick from dysentery that they could not function. As noted above, the only available "doctor" on board the ship as the battle got under way was one Usher Parsons, a 25 year old Surgeon's Mate (the equivalent of a Corpsman in today's navy). Parsons performed all the major emergency surgery during the battle and immediately thereafter. Those of the wounded, who were stabilized enough to be held overnight, were then operated on the next day on the main deck in with good lighting and fresh air.

Months after the battle, when the surgical outcome results were available, something startling was observed. The *Lawrence* crewmen had a much higher survival rate than had been recorded for any of the other naval engagements of the war. In fact, for

---

[3] It was traditional on small warships in naval engagements to transform the officer's wardroom into a surgery where the wounded were treated.

every wounded man upon whom Parsons operated, 96% survived, a record not matched until WWI, a hundred years later. An investigation was launched to try to identify what, if anything, Parsons had done that was different from what was done by the other ship surgeons.

One of Parson's practices, which no doubt made part of the difference, was that, when possible, he allowed the patient to stabilize overnight, which gave the patient time to regain strength and recover from the trauma of being wounded. Also, it allowed him to operate the next day in fresh air and bright daylight.

However, it was another new practice of his that is believed to have made the most difference. It turned out that Parsons had somewhere gotten the idea that, if the surgical instruments were warmed, it would be less traumatic to the patient. He accordingly had a pot of hot water on the ship's stove where he kept the instruments between procedures. Further, in order that the water not get clouded with debris from the instruments and have to be thrown out and new water continually heated, he insisted the instruments be rinsed clean after use and before re-immersion.

One can jump ahead in time and view what he had done in the context of modern sterilization science. We know today that dangerous organisms grow in the blood and tissue that inevitably remain on surgical instruments after use. We also know that these same organisms do not thrive on a clean, smooth metallic surface. (Even today, instruments run through an aggressive washing machine are actually sterile enough for many procedures).

It is true that it requires superheated steam to kill the most stubborn organisms, such as spores. It is also true, however, that most dangerous pathogens die at considerably lower temperatures. Parsons' washing and hot water procedure probably knocked out most of the "germs" that were causing the nosocomial infections which often occurred in battlefield wound surgery of the period.

Parsons therefore, between patients, was actually (and unwittingly) sterilizing, to a major degree, his surgical

35

instruments. (His concept of heating the instruments to reduce trauma, on the other hand, was never found to have that effect). He was doing the right thing for the wrong reason but his happy survivors did not mind.

Usher Parsons thus should be considered one of the heroes of the Battle of Lake Erie, as well as a pioneer in the field of sterilization, for all the lives he saved. It is an odd coincidence that Parsons, the accidental sterilization pioneer, sailed back to Erie, PA where, some 80 years later, the American Sterilizer Company, which went on to become the largest hospital sterilizer manufacturing plant in the world, was founded.

Appendix F has an account of Parson's distinguished career in medicine after he left the Navy

3. Perry's Last Battle

Perry went to sea at 13, as noted above. In his relatively short life, he fought in many major and bitterly-fought battles, on land as well as at sea, yet never received a life threatening wound. Perry certainly demonstrated good leadership and technical skills but he also was lucky. In the end, however, his luck ran out and he was finally brought down by an enemy he couldn't see.

Perry was sent to work out a coordinated effort to counteract piracy in the Caribbean. In 1819, while returning on the *USS Nonsuch* from a diplomatic mission to Venezuela to meet with Simon Bolivar, Perry contracted yellow fever. He died on his 34th birthday on August 23rd.

Chapter IV - "THREE STRIKES"

"We have met the Enemy and they are ours"
> Commodore Oliver Hazard Perry USN

"Make the best terms you can with the Americans. I am pulling out the British regulars and falling back to Kingston" This is the essence of the General Sheaffe's message to the townspeople and militia at York. (No record exists of the exact wording).
> General Roger Hale Sheaffe

"His Majesty's flag has not been tarnished"
> Commander Robert Barclay RN

"When your time comes to die, be not like those
whose hearts are filled with fear of death, so that
when their time comes they weep and pray for a little more time to
live their lives over again in a different way.
Sing your death song, and die like a hero going home"
> Tecumseh

Three American victories in the War of 1812 threw the British **"OUT"** of the "Old Northwest" (and in the process kept many of the future states between the Mississippi River and the Appalachians from possibly becoming part of Canada or an Indian Nation when the war ended). As noted later, the smashing of the Indian Confederation as part of this sequence of events meant that the Indians were not even represented at the peace negotiations. In turn the formerly British supported Indian resistance to the westward expansion of the United States was reduced.

A - STRIKE ONE – The Raid on York – April 1813

Due to divided loyalties on both sides of the border spying was very common. Families from the highest to the lowest levels of society were split. (Recall that the brother-in-law of Boston-born General Shaeffe, the British commander at York, was one of the signors of the Declaration of Independence!)

Through their spies, the British probably knew of the original plan to attack Kingston (and its shipyard). They therefore concentrated their fleet to protect Kingston. They learned too late that the Americans, reluctant to get into a major confrontation, had decided to raid lightly-defended York instead. As a result of this last minute switch, there was not a British warship within almost one hundred miles of York at the time of the raid.

American forces raided York (now Toronto) and destroyed the British naval base there. In so doing, they seized the twenty 24-pounder carronades that happened to be there. These carronades were on their way to be the principal battery of the *Detroit*, the British main ship for the upcoming Lake Erie battle, which was nearing completion at their base at Amherstburg.

As a result, instead of twenty identical guns using identical ammunition, the *Detroit* had to be equipped with a motley collection of mismatched, different caliber, cannon stripped from the nearby western British forts (two 24-pounder cannon, one 18-pounder cannon, six 12-pounder cannon, eight 9-pounder cannon, one 24-pounder carronade and one 18-pounder carronade) It will be evident later in this discussion why this change had serious consequences in the Battle of Lake Erie and the situation of the western British forts after that battle.

A second critical part of the naval supplies probably seized or destroyed in the raid were the flintlock firing mechanisms that facilitated the accurate timing in firing shipboard cannon. British warships of this period normally had these aids but none were found aboard the *Detroit* when it was captured (*See* Appendix C). This timing of firing is particularly important on

38

ships because normally the deck on which the cannon sit is constantly moving and so are the target ships. Ideally, the gun captain stands behind the cannon (but out of recoil range) and sights down the barrel. Without the convenience of these special mechanisms, the gun crew ass reduced to firing the cannon by standing next to the cannon and either using a match or firing a flintlock boarding pistol over gunpowder piled in the vent. The lack of gunlocks had serious consequences in the latter battle.

B -STRIKE TWO – The Battle of Lake Erie (aka the Battle of Put-in-Bay) – September 1813

Much has already been written about this battle. This discussion will focus on underreported aspects along with an analysis.

1. The Cannon Factors (See also Appendix B)

Perry might have suspected that the loss of the *Detroit's* intended carronades would force the British to switch over to the guns available from their forts, which were typically 6, 12 or (occasionally) 24-pounder long guns. He seems to have made his own armament decisions accordingly. Perry concentrated almost all his 32-pounder carronades on the *Lawrence* and the *Niagara*, which he intended to have fought broadside to broadside, and at close range against the two major British ships, the *Detroit* and the *Queen Charlotte*. (The only long guns on the *Lawrence* and *Niagara* were two 12-pounder "bow chasers" used in pursuits).

As noted, carronades require a smaller gun crew and have a higher rate of fire than the more awkward-to-reload long cannons. Long guns generally fire a smaller, higher velocity projectile. They require a larger gun crew than carronades.

Due to the combination of the mismatched guns and ammunition and the delay attendant to more manual type firing hampering the *Detroit*, the *Lawrence* or *Niagara* could and did deliver broadsides of considerably more pounds per minute of cannon balls compared to the *Detroit*. This is no doubt how the *Lawrence*, acting almost alone in the early part of the battle, was able to severely damage both of the main British ships and contribute to putting most of their officers out of action.

Perry placed almost all of his available large long guns on the smaller (mostly schooner rigged) vessels in his fleet. (*See* chart) These ships could never hope, and were not intended, to engage in broadsides against the *Detroit* or *Queen Charlotte*. However, they could maneuver more quickly and "point" higher upwind than big, square rigged brigs. Although these ships had comparatively fewer cannon, they were in most cases swivel-mounted to give them a wider angle of fire.

Barclay, on the other hand, had virtually all of his long guns on the *Detroit*. The Chart, Table I, shows the radical difference in the armament distribution between the two fleets. It is not noted in the literature whether the British distribution was a deliberate plan or simply the result of the *Detroit* being so late in completion that there was not enough time to restructure the armament assignments among the rest of his fleet.

TABLE I - Cannon Distribution Differences - Long Guns

Ship	24-32 Pounders	2-18 Pounders
USN		
Lawrence		2 -12s
Niagara		2 –12s
Ariel		4 –12s
Caledonia	2 – 24s	
Scorpion	1 - 32	
Porcupine	1 – 32	
Tigress	1 – 32	
Sommers	1 – 24	
Trippe	1 – 24	
TOTAL	7	8

Ship	24–32 Pounders	9-18 Pounders	2-6 Pounders
British RN			
Detroit	2 – 24s	1 – 18	
		6 – 12s	
		8 – 9s	
Queen Charlotte		3 -12s	
Little Belt		1 – 9	2 – 6
Lady Prevost		3 – 9s	
Chippewa		1 – 9	
Hunter			2 – 6s
			4 – 4s
			2 – 2s
TOTAL	2	23	10

Table II - Size of Cannonballs used in Three Strikes and Comparison with the Size of Current Balls used in Sports

Cannon Balls		Balls used in Sports	
Weight (lbs.)	Diameter (in.)	Sport	Diameter (in.)
2	2.44	Billiards	2.42
4	3.05	Baseball	2.94
6	3.49	Croquet	3.62
9	4.00	Softball	3.82
		Bocce	4.2
12	4.40	Shot Put	4.73
		Lawn Bowling	4.87
18	5.04		
24	5.55		
32	6.10		
		Volleyball	8.27

It is in the opening phases of the battle that the results of Strike One begin to show up. The initial good news for Barclay was that the numerous long guns with which the *Detroit* was equipped could be brought to bear at long range on the slowly approaching American fleet well before the British ships were in range of *Lawrence's* and *Niagara's* carronades.

One item of bad news for Barclay was that, without the precision in aiming and firing that the missing flintlock gunlocks would have provided, his ship's cannon fire on the American ships was somewhat inaccurate. Another problem his gunners initially faced was that they were firing down the line of the American fleet, which therefore presented a narrower target.

Barclay's third disadvantage was that, with two exceptions, all his long guns were medium or small caliber. As the Chart shows, when it came to heavy, long range artillery, he had only two 24 pounders (both on the *Detroit*) up against seven 24 and 32-pounder long guns distributed among six different ships of Perry's squadron. These seven big long range guns of Perry could deliver 288 pounds of cannon balls per salvo compared to Barclay's two delivering 48 pounds of cannon balls.

Even in the medium size 12-pounders Barclay was barely ahead (nine versus eight). The only cannon sizes where Barclay had a numerical advantage were the 2, 4 and 6-pounders (which are comparatively "pea shooters" in large ship naval warfare). As an example, the total broadside of all the guns on the British ship *Hunter,* which was only outfitted with these small guns, was only 30 pounds in total (less than just one of the *Lawrence's* 32-pounder carronades).

Therefore, when Perry in the *Lawrence* was beating upwind to engage the British fleet, and the *Detroit* opened fire on him with its long guns, Perry could order the closest gunboats (the *Scorpion*, the *Ariel* and the *Caledonia)* to return the fire with their long guns. They could do so without themselves getting too close to, or broadside of, the big British warships. In all probability

Perry directed them to concentrate their fire on the rigging of the *Detroit* and *Queen Charlotte*, using "chain shot"[4] as the range closed.

2. The Shadow of Impressment and Blockade

As noted previously, the Royal Navy was experiencing tremendous difficulty in continuing to staff their worldwide fleet of 740 warships with able seamen. When Commander Barclay took over the building, training and fighting of the British Lake Erie squadron, he found he had few trained sailors and gunners available. In spite of continual appeals, his commander, Commodore Yeo, would not spare him additional resources.

The blockade, which crippled American overseas trade, had some side effects. With few American merchantmen at sea, opportunities to impress seamen had dried up, further exacerbating Britain's manpower shortage. On the flip side, the blockade meant that there were many unemployed seamen in the major American east coast ports. The US Navy therefore was able to recruit a good number of experienced seamen to man Perry's fleet.

Years later, at Commander Barclay's court martial, Lieutenant Purvis of the *Detroit,* testified that, based on his conversation with the American officers after the battle; the *Lawrence* alone had more able bodied seamen aboard it than did the entire British squadron. Lieutenant Stokoe, of the *Queen Charlotte,* testified that only ten of that ship's crew of 130 were experienced sailors and only sixteen even including the "powder monkeys" (the young sailors who brought up the ammunition) were experienced gunners.

---

[4] Chain shot are two cannon balls fired from the same gun and tied together with a length of chain. This ammunition is designed to destroy the rigging on enemy vessels

3. The Three "Unsung Heroes"

Caledonia- Brig - two 24-pounder long guns and one 32-pounder carronade, all swivel-mounted.

Ariel – Schooner – four 12-pounder long guns

Scorpion – Schooner – one-32 pounder long gun and one 32-pounder carronade, both swivel-mounted.

    The ships and crews of these three smaller vessels were the unsung heroes of the fight. Everyone talks about the *Lawrence* and the *Niagara*, but these three played important roles.

    Back in the summer preceding the battle, Barclay's fleet (without the still incomplete *Detroit*) was reconnoitering Perry's activities at Presqu' Isle. It was these three ships (already outside the harbor entrance shoals themselves) that exchanged cannon fire with the British squadron. One lucky shot at the extreme ¾ mile range, probably from the *Scorpion,* damaged the rigging of the *Queen Charlotte*. In this incident, between the fire from these American ships and concern about staying out of the range of any American shore batteries on Presqu' Isle, Barclay apparently never got close enough to see that the *Lawrence* and the *Niagara* were not over the harbor entrance sand bar nor armed.

    In the Battle of Lake Erie itself, the little schooner *Scorpion*, with a crew size one-third that of the *Niagara*, suffered as many killed as the *Niagara*. The *Scorpion*, which was at the head of, and had one of the largest long guns in the whole fleet, fired the first American shot in the Battle. Later, in pursuit of the small British ships trying to flee after the battle and to force them to strike their colors, the *Scorpion* fired the last shot, as well. The *Scorpion*'s acting Captain, Stephen Champlin, was Perry's cousin.

    Early in the Battle, Finnis, the Captain of the *Queen Charlotte* saw that his intended adversary, the *Niagara*, was hanging way back. He closed up to just astern of the *Detroit* so that both British main ships could pound the *Lawrence* with their broadsides. At this juncture, it was not the *Niagara* (as many people think) that first tried to come to the aid of the *Lawrence*. It was the small three-gun brig *Caledonia* who followed just behind the *Lawrence* into the British line, engaging the *Queen Charlotte* "at half pistol shot range."

At Commander Barclay's court martial, Lt. Stokoe of the *Queen Charlotte,* when asked whether the principal damage to his ship was from the *Niagara*, testified *No, from the Caledonia who laid on our beam with two long 24-pounders on pivots, also out of (our) carronades' shot distance.*

Captain Turner, on the *Caledonia*, knew he could not match the *Queen Charlotte* broadside for broadside. Therefore, he came up on the port side of the *Queen Charlotte*, but slightly astern so that the *Queen Charlotte* could not bring her broadside facing guns to bear. The *Caledonia*'s guns, however, were all on swivel mounts; so Turner could, with relative impunity, have his guns fire diagonally down the deck of the *Queen Charlotte*. The *Scorpion's* guns were also swiveled.

The heavily-damaged *Lawrence* was losing way so that the *Detroit* and *Queen Charlotte* were pulling gradually ahead, approaching the point where the *Caledonia* would be between them and the *Lawrence*. Therefore, between its own bulk and the smoke from its cannons, the *Caledonia* probably screened some of Perry's historic longboat transfer to the *Niagara* from the gunners and marines of the *Queen Charlotte*.

The rigging damage to the main British ships from the cannon fire from these three ships throughout the whole time of the engagement may very well have been a contributing factor to the difficulties in maneuvering which culminated in the bowsprits of the *Detroit* and *Queen Charlotte* becoming tangled. Significantly, in the report of Barclay, the British commander, he states that the *Detroit* "...was a perfect wreck principally from the* *raking fire of the Gunboats* (he was referring to the schooners *Ariel* and *Porcupine* and the small brig *Caledonia* which had all engaged his flagship). After the battle, Perry particularly commended Captain Turner of the *Caledonia* for his actions and the actions of his crew during the battle. James Fennimore Cooper, in his *History of the US Navy*, also notes Turner's action.

Brig USS *Caledonia*

Most of Perry's and Barclay's ships, which were built hastily in a few months from whatever (green) timber was available, rotted in a few years. The *Caledonia* was built as a merchant ship in peacetime (1807) of the proper seasoned timber. After the war, she continued her career as a merchant ship until 1835 when she was dismantled for salvage. The *Caledonia* built for cargo capacity and not for speed, easily carried and effectively used two 24-pounder long guns and a 32-pounder carronade (all swivel mounted). The total weight of these three guns with their carriages, but not including the swivel platforms, was 14,000 pounds. Since she had not been built as a warship, however, she lacked quarters[5] to shield the crew from musket fire and grapeshot.

---

[5] The raised bulwarks on warships

47

Pictured above is a reconstruction of a topsail schooner similar to the USS *Ariel*, second ship in the line of battle at the Battle of Lake Erie The actual *Ariel* had a displacement of 75 tons and carried four 12 pounder long guns. With her long guns she was able to return fire when the *Detroit* commenced firing on the approaching American fleet.

The *Ariel*, together with the *Scorpion* and the *Caledonia* was equipped with long guns that could reach the oncoming British fleet. Perry's brigs, the *Lawrence* and the *Niagara* were equipped for the most part with large, but shorter range, carronades.

C - STRIKE THREE - Battle of the Thames – October 1813

1. The Situation at Fort Amherstburg

When the Americans seized the *Detroit*'s intended armament, the British were forced to strip the forts at Detroit and Amherstburg of most of their cannon to equip the *Detroit*, leaving the forts more vulnerable to attack. A major contingent of the British troops stationed at the forts had been pressed into service as marines (and were subsequently captured by the Americans). The forts were therefore also undermanned.

The Americans' new control of Lake Erie meant that Fort Amherstburg and other British western forts could not be resupplied or reinforced. The regular troops and sailors already were on half rations. To exacerbate matters, also assembled at the forts were a large number of warriors (and families) of the Six Nation Confederation (Mohawks, Oneida, Tuscarora, Onondaga, Cayuga and Seneca), under the leadership of their leader Tecumseh, who had come there to fight alongside the British. The Indians were, however, rapidly eating up the food supplies.

2. The Decision to Fall Back

British General Procter originally had wanted to fall back all the way to the strong British position at Burlington Heights, at Lake Ontario's west end. However, Tecumseh remonstrated with him over the commitments that the King (through his representatives) had made to the Confederation in return for their support. (*See* Tecumseh's letter to Procter in Appendix E)

Ultimately, Procter decided to abandon the forts and retreat up the Thames River which ran east (toward Burlington Heights). He committed to finding a place on the Thames River where he and the Indian allies could stop and make a stand against the pursuing American army. He chose Moraviantown (which he felt might be far enough east so that supplies and reinforcements from Burlington Heights might ultimately be able to reach him).

3. The American Land Offensive

General Harrison and his army of US regulars and Kentucky militiamen were, for the most part, ferried over Lake Erie and then continually supplied by Perry's fleet as they chased Proctor's army up the Thames River. At Moraviantown, the Americans caught up with the half-starved British regulars and their disgruntled Indian allies. After a short battle, most of the British troops were taken prisoner. Tecumseh was killed and, without his leadership, the Indian Confederation fell apart. Some of the Indians sought refuge at Burlington Heights; most simply went home.

D - The Battle of Lake Ontario that Never Was

1. The Navy Portion

The precursor for the Three Strikes and their aftermath was the massive arms race for a naval battle that never took place. When the war broke out, both sides had mostly converted merchant ships and not much in the way of warships on Lake Ontario. The British set up shipyards at their main naval base at Kingston and a smaller base at York. The Americans set up their shipyard at Sackett's Harbor, New York. Both sides launched into a shipbuilding race.

In the end, the campaign on Lake Ontario was a "carpenter's war". For most of the war, the British Commander for the Great Lakes (with most of his attention on Lake Ontario operations) was Sir James Yeo. The American Commander for the Great Lakes (also with most of his attention on Lake Ontario) was Isaac Chauncey.

With one minor exception, noted below, the two Lake Ontario fleets never met in battle during the entire war. At the end of the war, the Americans had eight major warships on the Lake (ranging in size from 243 to 1,580 tons displacement) and the British nine (ranging in size from 187 to 2,305 tons displacement). Both sides had three additional ships under construction, two of which, on both sides, were over 2,000 tons in displacement.

The Chart shows the total armament of the two fleets. The ships of both of the Lake Ontario fleets were far larger and far more heavily armed ships than the ships of the Lake Erie fleets. Perry's largest ship, *Niagara,* was only 493 tons displacement and armed with eighteen "32-pounder" carronades and two "12-pounder" long guns and Barclay's flagship. The British *Detroit,* was only 305 tons displacement and armed with 18 various size long guns ranging from "9-pounders" to "24-pounders" plus a single "24- pounder" carronade.

Except for a few minor skirmishes, the largest of which is described below, the War of 1812 on Lake Ontario consisted of one long "Cold War". Both sides spent the entire war building larger and larger ships requiring major commitment of their scarce resources in ship rigging and armament as well as able-bodied seamen. The magnitude of the madness is best illustrated by the fact that, by 1816, five of the largest warships in the entire world would have been sailing on small, landlocked, Lake Ontario.

The war in this particular theatre was a standoff. However, in the broader context of the Three Strikes, diversion of resources in preparation for what was anticipated to be the decisive Battle of Lake Ontario was probably a major factor in the British defeat at the Battle of Lake Erie. The diversion of resources probably also was a factor in the British defeat in the 1814 Battle of Lake Champlain.

2. The Army Portion

General Francis Rottenburg, the Commander of Upper Canada steadfastly refused to send troops to Lake Erie to destroy the

American shipyard and ships under construction at Erie, PA. Procter and Barclay pleaded their case that this move would guarantee British mastery of the upper Great Lakes. They were quite possibly right since the American Erie base at Presqu' Isle was very lightly defended in the summer of 1813.

Rottenburg was more concerned about defending the British shipyards/bases on Lake Ontario and accumulating forces to attach the American shipyard/base at Sackett's Harbor on Lake Ontario than in (to him) the minor Lake Erie confrontation. So, the British land actions, that might have broken the "Three Strike" sequence, never happened due to the preoccupation by both sides with Lake Ontario.

Figure 2. American and British Fleets on Lake Ontario

a. Cannons on the US Ships at War's End
Carronades
> Sixty six 42-pounders
> Fourteen 32-pounders
> Twenty eight 24-pounders

Long guns
> Fifty two 32–pounders
> Twenty eight 24-pounders
> Two 18-pounders
> Ten 12-pounders

Cannons on US Ships under Construction at War's End
Carronades
> Two hundred sixty (primarily) 42-pounders

b. Cannon on British Ships on Lake Ontario at War's End
Carronades
> Ten 64-pounders
> Forty two 32-pounders
> Twelve 24-pounders

Long guns
> Twenty eight 32-pounders
> One hundred five 24-pounders
> Eighteen 18-pounders
> Ten 12-pounders

Cannon on British Ships under Construction at War's End
Carronades
> Seventy six 32-pounders

Long guns
> Thirty six 32-pounders

As far as Strike Two is concerned, American, British and Canadian historians have argued that Yeo achieved the Lake Ontario standoff at such a cost that other operations were curtailed or thwarted. For example, as noted above, Yeo's hoarding of men and supplies, and failure to forward sufficient of these to the British squadron on Lake Erie, probably contributed to the British defeat. As noted elsewhere, at Barclay's court martial, Lt. Purvis of the *Detroit* testified that, in conversations with American officers after the Battle of Lake Erie, he was able to determine that the Americans had more able-bodied seaman on the *Lawrence* alone than Barclay had in his entire fleet. The single largest of Yeo's Lake Ontario ships required almost twice as many seamen in its crew as Barclay's entire fleet needed.

The British Navy worldwide was desperately short of seamen (hence impressment). The Canadian Maritime provinces, with no blockade, had every sailor they could find manning their

53

merchant and fishing fleets. By contrast, the Americans, with their merchant ships blockaded, had plenty of seamen available.

The largest of several (indecisive) encounters between the Lake Ontario fleets during the war, happened on the western end of that lake when, on 28 September 1813, they met, quite by accident, in York Bay. Chauncey actually was there covering a proposed movement of the American army from the Niagara area to Sacket's Harbor, while Yeo had just delivered supplies to the British forces on the Niagara peninsula.

Both squadrons spotted each other early in the morning. Yeo headed south in a heavy wind, ahead and to leeward of the American fleet. Chauncey had become exasperated by the poor sailing qualities of some of his schooners, and as a result, his three fastest vessels (the *General Pike*, the *Sylph* and the *Madison*) were actually towing the schooners *Asp*, *Ontario* and *Fair American*.

At about 12:40 pm, Yeo abruptly reversed course, apparently intending to exchange a single broadside with *General Pike* while they passed on opposite tacks, and then concentrate fire against the weaker schooners at the rear of Chauncey's line. However, Chauncey also reversed course and the *General Pike* and Yeo's flagship, the *Wolfe*, exchanged several broadsides.

The American fire brought down *Wolfe*'s mizzenmasts and main-topmasts. The *Royal George* interposed itself between the *Wolfe* and the *General Pike* while the crew of the *Wolfe* cleared away the wreckage. Both the British ships, followed by the rest of Yeo's squadron, headed downwind towards Burlington Bay and the safety of the shore batteries defending the approach to the British base at Burlington Heights, at the western end of the lake. With the British having lost the entire Lake Erie fleet just two weeks prior, Yeo, probably and understandably, was not of a mind to take any risks with the Lake Ontario fleet at this time.

For a while, however, the two squadrons were exchanging broad-sides, and Chauncey's officers urged him to capture the two rearmost British vessels (the *Beresford* and the *Melville*) to at least

54

get something out of the battle. Instead, Chauncey reportedly exclaimed "All or none" and led his ships off in pursuit of the *Wolfe,* the *Royal George* and the other lead British ships. He refused to cast off the towlines, however, so the American fleet could not sail fast enough to catch the British ships. Two small American schooners trailing the American line, inexplicably had never reversed course with the rest of the fleet, and were captured.

After a chase lasting ninety minutes, Yeo dropped anchor off the north shore of Burlington Bay. The wind had risen to a gale, the American squadron had straggled, and the *General Pike* herself had received damage. Chauncey called off the action, stating officially that he felt that, if he had tried to continue the attack, the American squadron might be driven ashore, into British-held territory.

E - "OUT" – Strategic Consequences

After the Three Strikes, the British never again gained control from Lake Ontario and westward and were not in a position to lay claim to any American territory in any of what are now the US Midwestern states, in the peace negotiations. (*See* the Duke of Wellington's analysis of the subsequent military situation.)

If the British and their Indian Allies had been successful in these three encounters and were in effective control of the portion of North America which stretched from the Appalachian Mountains to the Mississippi River, they could have invoked the principle of *"uti possidetis"* at the treaty table.[6] However, the British and Indians instead were defeated in each of the Three

---

[6] *Uti possidetis* (Latin for "as you possess") is a principle in international law that territory and other property remains with its possessor at the end of a conflict, unless otherwise provided for by treaty; if such a treaty does not include conditions regarding the possession of property and territory taken during the war, then the principle of *uti possidetis* will prevail. Originating in Roman law, the phrase is derived from the Latin expression *uti possidetis, ita possideatis,* meaning "may you continue to possess such as you do possess" (lit., "as you possess, thus may you possess"). This principle enables a belligerent party to claim territory that it has acquired by war. This principle was affirmed by the International Court of Justice as recently as the 1986 Case *Burkina-Faso v. Mali.*

Strikes. Thus, under international law, they had no legal right to claim territory which they no longer controlled. (*See* Wellington quote Chapter V.D)

The Indian Confederation, which before October 1813 had supplied a significant portion of the British fighting forces (at relatively small cost to England), was now essentially gone for the balance of the war. To continue the war meant transporting over, at great cost, large numbers of Redcoats to replace the Indians. (16,000 reinforcements arrived in Canada in late 1813.)

After many years of fighting the French (at great expense), the British public had had enough and were balking at more taxes to support the conflict with America. In addition, the seemingly increasingly "no win" American conflict was a distraction to the much more important Congress of Vienna, which was winding up the settlement after the Napoleonic wars.

As is detailed in Chapter VI, in the Peace negotiations, the British eventually were forced to renege on their promised commitment to an Indian Homeland. Without British support of their territorial claims and without unifying leadership, the Six Tribe Confederation never again acted as a "nation" and the tribes were gradually and relentlessly forced from their lands. As noted earlier, the Indian Confederation was not even represented at the Peace Conference. The Canadian Indians, who had also trusted in the promises of the Crown to guarantee their territorial integrity, apparently did not fare much better over the years.

Chapter V - Luck and the "Three Strikes"

"Trouble no one about his religion"
                    and
"Respect others in their views and demand that they respect yours"

                                        Tecumseh

No amount of careful planning can beat pure luck. - Anonymous

Luck is what happens when preparation meets opportunity --
                                        Seneca

A -Luck and Strike One – The Raid on York

1. How York was chosen as the target

On January 13, 1813, John Armstrong, Jr. was appointed United States Secretary of War. Having served as a soldier, he quickly appreciated the situation on Lake Ontario, and devised a plan by which by April 1 a force of 7,000 regular soldiers would be concentrated at Sackett's Harbor. Working together with the Lake Ontario squadron commanded by Commodore Chauncey[7], this force would capture the major base at Kingston before the Saint Lawrence River thawed and substantial British reinforcements could arrive. Loss of the Royal Naval Dockyard together with many of the vessels of the Provincial Marine would make almost every British post west of Kingston vulnerable, if not untenable.

Armstrong, in February, conferred with Major General Henry Dearborn. Both Dearborn and Chauncey agreed with Armstrong's plan at this point. Subsequently they had second thoughts when they learned that Lieutenant General Sir George Prevost the British Governor General of Canada, had travelled up

---

[7] Perry reported to Chauncey.

the frozen Saint Lawrence to visit Upper Canada. This visit was made necessary because Major General Roger Hale Sheaffe, who had succeeded Brock as Lieutenant Governor of Upper Canada, was ill and unable to perform his various duties. Prevost was actually accompanied by only small detachments of reinforcements. Nevertheless, both Chauncey and Dearborn believed that Prevost's arrival indicated an imminent attack on Sackett's Harbor, and reported that Kingston now had a garrison of 6,000 or more British regulars.

Even though Prevost soon returned to Lower Canada, and deserters and pro-American Canadian civilians subsequently reported that the true size of Kingston's garrison was 600 regulars and 1,400 militia, Chauncey and Dearborn chose to use the earlier inflated figure to justify a change in plan. In fairness, up to this point in the war, most American incursions into Canada had been disasters and these two were going to be cautious unless they were sure of overwhelming superiority in numbers and artillery support.

Furthermore, even though two brigades of troops under Brigadier General Zebulon Pike had arrived to reinforce the troops already at Sackett's Harbor, the number of effective troops available to Dearborn fell far short of the 7,000 originally planned, mainly as a result of sickness. During March, Chauncey and Dearborn recommended to Armstrong that, when the ice on the lake thawed, they should instead attack the smaller and less well-defended British base at York (today's Toronto) instead.

Although York was the provincial capital of Upper Canada, it was considered far less important than Kingston as a military objective. Armstrong, by now back in Washington, acquiesced in this change of plan as he believed that Dearborn might well have better local information.

2. The Luck of the Misdirected Regulars

When the American invasion fleet was sighted and the British realized a landing was imminent, General Sheaffe, who was in command at York, ordered a company of the Glengarry Light Infantry to support the Ojibwa (Appendix J) and Mississauga Indian allies who had been sent to repel the American landing. However, these newly arrived Redcoats were not familiar with the area and they possibly became lost in the town outskirts.

Some sources claim these troops may have been deliberately misdirected by Major-General Æneas Shaw, the Adjutant General of the Canadian Militia. It is alleged that he may have diverted the regulars so they would end up reinforcing the relatively few of his own militia (who had been assigned to protect the north flank) that he had been able to muster. In fairness to Shaw, he had not seen combat for 32 years and was fatally ill at this time. (He died less than a year after the battle). Whatever the reason, the regulars never arrived at the beachhead.

The American fleet, consisting of a corvette, a brig and twelve schooners, provided covering fire to the landings using large cannon loaded primarily with grapeshot. The Indians were experienced and brave fighters but they had little training or experience in fighting where the trees they were accustomed to using for cover were being torn to flying splinters. Without the support of the regulars, who were trained in fighting under such heavy artillery fire, the Indians fell back and the entire American army landed safely with minimum losses.

It is likely the Americans, who had the British outnumbered and outgunned would have prevailed eventually but the luck of having no regular troops at the beach-head made the capture of York much easier.

3. What the Americans discovered when they captured The
York Naval Base

Canada at this point in history had very little industrial capability
to produce the equipment needed to outfit naval vessels. As a
result, almost all the equipment for the new British corvette, the
Detroit, then nearing completion at the British naval base and
dockyard in Amherstburg, had to be shipped from England. The
Detroit, with a planned battery of twenty 24-pounder carronades
was to be the flagship of the Lake Erie squadron which fleet would
continue the British dominance of Lake Erie and protect the
supply route to all Britain's western forts and outposts.

When the Americans searched the base they discovered,
much to their surprise, the carronades which were in route to
Amherstburg. Almost as important, they found the flintlock
gunlock firing mechanisms (*see* Appendix B) intended for all
these cannon. All British warships of this era were equipped with
these mechanisms, which permitted far more precise firing timing
(a major advantage when firing from pitching and rolling decks
with a moving target).

4. The impact of this "Stroke of Luck" on the Battle of Lake Erie"

When news of the disaster reached the shipyard at Amherstburg
they had no choice but to outfit the *Detroit* with fortress cannon
stripped from the western forts. Instead of twenty matching
carronades, the *Detroit* ended up with an assortment of different
guns. (Imagine the confusion of the mostly-inexperienced gun
crews during battle when faced with four different size cannon
balls and six different size powder bags!).

Reloading long cannon normally required a gun crew of
12, whereas carronades required smaller crews. The *Detroit* was
already desperately short of experienced gunners and manning all
these long guns instead of the (smaller crew) intended carronades

exacerbated the problem. Long guns also took longer to reload compared to carronades, reducing the anticipate rate of fire.

The long guns were much heavier than the carronades. For instance, a 24-pounder long gun weighed about 6,000 pounds (3 tons), triple the weight of a similar caliber carronade. All this extra weight mounted high in the hull reduced seaworthiness and maneuverability, particularly with converted merchant vessels.

When Perry, in the *Lawrence*, with his eighteen fast-firing 32-pounder carronades finally engaged the *Detroit* and the *Lady Charlotte* (with her fourteen 24-pounder carronades and three 24-pounder long guns) he was able to deliver almost as many pounds of iron cannon balls per minute as the two British ships combined.

By the time the *Lawrence's* guns were finally all silenced, the senior officers on both these two main British ships were all wounded or dead. The ships themselves had been rendered unmaneuverable, their rigging in tatters and their bowsprits entangled. The *Lawrence* itself was a smoldering wreck. However, her sister ship, the *Niagara*, which had missed much of the heaviest firing, was relatively undamaged and was able to sail up and force the surrender of the British squadron.

Had the *Detroit* been outfitted with its originally intended artillery and proper advanced firing mechanisms, the serendipitous one-two punch of the *Lawrence, Caledonia and the other gunboats* beating up the two main British ships to the point where the *Niagara* could finish things off, might not have worked.

B -Luck and Strike Two – The Battle of Lake Erie

1 – Luck and the Caledonia

The *Caledonia* was a sturdy small brig that the British had purchased and converted to a warship. It was anchored off Fort Erie when it was captured by an American raiding party let by Lt. Elliott (later the much-maligned initial captain of the *Niagara* See

61

Appendix H). The Americans succeeded in getting the vessel safely to the American base at Black Rock. There it was trapped, since to try to leave would expose it to British gunners across the Niagara River in Fort Erie.

The next lucky break was that the British were driven from Fort George (downstream on the Niagara River at Newark) and were therefore forced to abandon Fort Erie. Seeing the opportunity, Perry came down from Erie, took command of the *Caledonia* and four other smaller ships which also had been trapped at Black Rock.

Perry was successful in sneaking this small squadron down the lake to the safety of the Erie harbor to join the fleet he was assembling. Perry's famous luck held because a fog came up that allowed him to slip into the Erie harbor undetected.

b) Perry was lucky to have *Caledonia* at the Battle of Lake Erie. It is obvious from the description of the Battle of Lake Erie in the "Strike 2" section of this book, that the brig *Caledonia* was a significant player. Her two long range 24-pounder cannon returned the fire of the long range guns on the *Detroit* as the American fleet closed and later alone first came to the aid of the *Lawrence* which was embattled with the *Detroit* and the *Queen Charlotte*. *Caledonia's* gun smoke may have helped screen Perry's skiff as he was rowed from the *Lawrence* to the *Niagara*.

Barclay conceded in his report that much of the damage to the rigging of both his main ships was inflicted by *the gunboats"* (*Ariel, Scorpion* and *Caledonia*). The resultant unmanageability of the two British ships no doubt contributed to their collision.

2 – Luck of the Lady from Amherstburg

Throughout the summer of 1813, Barclay's fleet (less the *Detroit,* which was still under construction) maintained a blockade and surveillance of the entrance to Erie harbor. Since the port of Erie was familiar to his Canadian Lake Erie sailors, Barclay knew that the Erie harbor entrance was relatively shallow.

Barclay realized that in order to get the *Lawrence* and the *Niagara* across the bar Perry was going to have to use extreme measures to lighten both ships.. His hope was to be able to attack these two main ships when were being slowly brought through the shallow, winding entrance and destroy or severely cripple them.

Barclay had to routinely abandon his position to go back to base and re-provision. Perry monitored this pattern very closely and then, just at the right time, got lucky again. The British fleet was away longer than usual. And, as in many cases in history, the "luck" is said to have involved a lady. Captain Barclay has been criticized for pausing in his blockade overlong on this occasion. Although there is some controversy about the role of the lady, it seems to be corroborated in Mrs. Amelia Harris's "Memoirs of her father and the early settlement of Long Point" who wrote:

When the weather was too rough for the blockading squadron to remain outside the harbour, it was also too rough for the American fleet to get over the bar; consequently we felt very safe. During this summer of 1813, Captain Barclay used to have private information – not very reliable, as the result proved – of what progress Perry's ships were making in the yards. He used to occasionally leave the blockade and go to Amherstburg and Ryerse (near present Port Dover) for supplies.

The Americans took note of this, and made plans and preparations accordingly. On one of his resupply trips to his home port, Barclay was introduced to an attractive widow of a high ranking British officer, visiting in Amherstburg. She was most anxious to get back to York.

Captain Barclay offered her passage and brought her to Ryerse (near present day Port Dover), from where there was a coach to enable continued travel east. Upon arrival he escorted her to Dr. Ralph's home, (apparently an acquaintance of her former husband). The townspeople, appreciative of Barclay's courtesy, invited him and his officers to remain for a banquet the next day.

Thanks to this delay, when the British fleet came back in sight of Erie the following day, they saw, to their great distress, all the American fleet now armed and riding safely at anchor outside the bar. Since the American fleet now had them outgunned and had more real warships, the British broke off the blockade and headed back to Amherstburg and their newly launched *Detroit*.[8]

No one could have fought more bravely at the subsequent battle than Captain Barclay. At the same time, those who knew of his abandoning his blockade for so long could not help feeling that part of the disaster lay at his door. There is no controversy about Perry's "luck" in having extra time to execute the complicated process of dragging the two larger ships (stripped of all armaments and other removable gear) across the shallows blocking the harbor entrance using "camels" (pontoons).

3 – The Luck of the wind on the 9th.

Barclay set sail from Amherstburg on the evening of September 12th to engage Perry. His plan was to sail, under cover of darkness, the thirty-some miles to Put-in-Bay on South Bass Island where Perry's fleet was at anchor. Put-in-Bay is an excellent harbor, but it is surrounded by many small islands and shoals. Barclay

---

[8] If the story is true, Barclay's actions were not unprecedented. The importance to British Officers of this era of conducting themselves as "gentlemen" is also illustrated by a situation that is said to have occurred at British Fort George across from American Fort Niagara, where the Niagara River empties into Lake Ontario. Between the wars, in this semi wilderness region, there was little to do on these remote posts. The officers got in the habit of regularly rowing across the river to dine together. The story goes that they were just sitting down to dinner when word was received that America and Britain were at war. The British commandant announced that "there was no sense letting a little unpleasantness ruin a good dinner." They finished the meal and the American officers rowed back across. See also Appendix I

planned to arrive at dawn and attack the American fleet as it tried to get maneuvering room.

As luck would have it, the breeze that night was unusually light and he made unexpectedly slow progress. When dawn broke (and the American lookouts spotted them), the British fleet was still over ten miles off and the element of surprise had been lost. The American fleet had time to raise anchor, clear the harbor and sail out to meet the British.

4 - The Luck of the Wind on the 10th

When the British fleet was bearing down on Put-in-Bay from the northwest it had the advantage of a breeze coming from the southwest. Barclay therefore had the wind on his beam and his ships were sailing on a broad reach. Under these conditions, his ships had maximum speed and maneuverability.

Wind from this direction was Perry's worst nightmare. In order to come out of the harbor and head west so he could simultaneously get clear of the surrounding islands and try to get to the windward of Barclay, he had to tack into the wind. Square-rigged sailing ships with shallow draft (like the *Lawrence* and the *Niagara*) make very slow progress beating upwind.

Perry's fleet was able to pass to the south of Snake Island but Barclay was closing and he was running out of time to get any further west. Perry therefore headed northeast. In this circumstance, Perry's "Luck of Strike One" was not so lucky. As noted above, the *Detroit* had ended up with virtually all long guns. The *Detroit* turned toward the west (broadside to the American fleet) and began to pound Perry's up-coming ships at long range. The *Lawrence*, equipped primarily with shorter range (and broadside firing) carronades, could not return fire and just had to take it as the American fleet closed, maddeningly slowly. The schooners *Scorpion* and *Ariel* which were ahead of the *Lawrence* in the American line and the small brig *Caledonia* which was immediately astern of the *Lawrence*, were better off. They were all equipped with long guns and were at least able to return fire.

Perry's luck then returned. The wind suddenly veered around to come from the south. Perry now had the wind abeam. He was sailing on a broad reach and his fleet began to close the gap more rapidly. The *Lawrence* was soon able to bring its broadside of 32-pound carronades to bear on the *Detroit*. The smaller American gunboats could now maneuver outside the *Detroit's* angle of fire and concentrate on destroying its rigging and that of the arriving *Queen Charlotte* as well. Barclay lost his ability to dictate the location and direction of the battle line.

The change in wind direction had a further benefit to the Americans. In 1813, there was no such thing as smokeless powder. Wind from the south and at close range would have blown all the smoke from the American cannon into the eyes of the British gunners. As noted previously, this also might have helped obscure the skiff transferring Perry from the *Lawrence* to the *Niagara*.

The *Lawrence* temporarily regained the advantage, until the *Queen Charlotte*, perceiving that its assigned opponent. the *Niagara*, was inexplicably hanging back (half a mile astern?), moved up the British line to just behind the *Detroit* and joined her in pounding the *Lawrence*. This action was not enough, however. Between the damage from the *Lawrence*, the *Scorpion*, the *Ariel* and the *Caledonia*, and with all senior officers killed or wounded, the *Detroit* and the *Queen Charlotte* collided and became "dead in the water".

5. Luck and the wind on the 11th

After the battle, the American sailors and some paroled British seamen worked all afternoon and through the night getting the *Lawrence*, the *Detroit* and the *Queen Charlotte* repaired to the point where they could be sailed. On the morning of the 11th the fleet got under way with a very favorable wind and by the early afternoon was at anchor in the harbor at Put-in-Bay. This is a fairly good size harbor but had never before (or possibly never since) been pressed to accommodate 15 large "tall ships".

Perry was once again lucky, this time in getting his fleet safely in harbor on the 11th because that night a strong gale blew through western Lake Erie. The fleet escaped damage, except that the *Queen Charlotte* dragged its anchor and (hard to believe) once again collided with, and tangled rigging with, the *Detroit*. The temporary fixes did not hold up and the masts and spars of both ships were heavily damaged.

C - Luck and Strike Three – Battle of Moraviantown

1. The Early 1800s English Involvement with the Indians

One of the factors that induced those portions of the United States, that were extending settlement over the mountains, to support a Declaration of War against England were the increasingly violent attacks by the Indians. There was plenty of evidence that the British were trading arms and ammunition for furs to the Indians, particularly those west of the Appalachian Mountains.

The English were concerned about westward expansion of the United States for a number of reasons. With the entire western half of Canada virtually uninhabited and with the easiest access to western Canada being to go through the U. S. south of the Great Lakes, rather than the northern route across Upper Canada, they feared an eventual American takeover of western Canada.

The British did not want the upstart colonies (States) to colonize the land between the Appalachians and the Mississippi River or grow any bigger or stronger. Their long range thinking was made clear by the pre-Revolution Quebec Act of 1774 which had Quebec extending south to the Ohio River and west to the Mississippi River. The Act envisioned an Indian Nation south of the Ohio River and east of the Mississippi River and south to the

Florida border (as a buffer state). British paranoia about the expansion of their former colonies was exacerbated with the Americans 1803 purchase of the Louisiana Territory from France.

The British were big players in and benefited greatly from the fur trade with the Indians in this region. The British had good reason to be very liberal in trading guns for furs with the Indians because the Indians then could use their newfound military might to raid western settler's homes and villages.

2. America's Luck comes to Moraviantown

After the Americans captured the nine British vessels in Barclay's fleet they now had 15 armed warships on Lake Erie where the British had none. The Americans were in strong control of Lake Erie making resupply of the western British forts very difficult.

In Amherstburg, General Procter now had a dilemma. Tecumseh and thousands of his warriors (and their families in many cases) were encamped at the fort and rapidly going through the remaining food supply. He already had placed the British regulars and seamen on half rations. The forts in the region had all been stripped of their guns to equip the *Detroit*, as discussed earlier. Having sent about 150 regulars to serve as marines on the fleet, he only had 800 of the 41st Foot Regiment left at the forts.

General Procter decided to destroy the forts and any remaining ships and retreat up the Thames River, planning to fall back toward the strong British base at Burlington Heights at the west end of Lake Ontario. The Indian chiefs were very angry. They perceived the British withdrawals as reneging on the promises the Crown had made to them. Only 500 warriors agreed to come with Tecumseh as he accompanied Procter's army eastward. The rest of his Indians probably headed home.

The veterans of the 1st Battalion of the had 41st had been serving in Upper Canada since the start of the war, and had suffered heavy casualties in several engagements during 1813 (including the Battle of Lake Erie, in which men of the regiment served aboard Barclay's ships and had been killed or captured.

By contrast, General Harrison's fresh force numbered at least 3,500 infantry and cavalry. He had a small detachment of regulars from the 27th US Infantry and five brigades of Kentucky militia led by Isaac Shelby, the 63-year-old governor of Kentucky and a hero of the American Revolutionary War. He also had 1,000 volunteer cavalry under Colonel Richard Mentor Johnson. Most were from Kentucky.

The Thames runs east-west parallel to the shore of Lake Erie to its south. Perry was able to ferry over most of General Harrison's army (some came by land) and then keep it supplied from his ships. Some of his shallow draft ships traveled up the Thames as far as feasible in support. The others followed up north shore of Lake Erie. What could not have been predicted was that one of Harrison's men was carrying in his bullet pouch one of the luckiest bullets of the war, from the American viewpoint.

At Moraviantown, Harrison's troops caught up with Proctor's column and after a short skirmish between the half starved British foot soldiers and the well-trained Kentucky cavalry, most of the regulars surrendered. The Kentucky riflemen fought the Indians in individual combat through the adjoining swamps and eventually prevailed over them as well. In the fighting, that lucky bullet killed Tecumseh. Without his leadership and unifying abilities, the Confederacy began to fall apart. Although a few of the Shawnee made it to Burlington with the remnants of Procter's army, all across Canada and the US most of the Confederacy's Indian fighters began to drift home.

D. the Luck of having the Duke of Wellington's Assessment benefit the American's side in Peace Negotiations

When considering where the Duke of Wellington was coming from as he followed and commented on, the campaign in North

America, it may helpful to draw a parallel to General Eisenhower and the invasion of Europe in WWII. Both of these Generals, in addition to their military prowess, were masters of logistics and logistics was one of the key success factors in both instances. Time and again you will see Wellington pointing out that, with little in the way of local resources, supplies to support the armies must be brought long distances. Furthermore, in North America for the last several hundred miles, the only feasible routes were over waters currently firmly controlled by the Americans.

Starting in February 1813, Wellington warned Bathurst, Secretary of State for War and the Colonies, that expansion of the American war would complicate matters in the war against Napoleon on the Continent and that, therefore, the leadership in North America: *(Prevost) should not `be induced by any hopes of trifling advantages to depart from a strong defensive system,'"* *and that such offensives "would only weaken him, and ... augment the spirits and hopes of the enemy.* To Wellington, the American war served the interests of France by forcing Britain to split her resources between two continents and this diversion might even ultimately have created a division between Britain and her allies.

In February 1814, just before Wellington's final peninsular offensive, Bathurst invited Wellington to update his assessment of events in America. *The defense of Canada,* Wellington wrote in reply*, depends upon the navigation of the lakes ... Any offensive operation founded upon Canada must be preceded by the establishment of naval superiority on the lakes.*(At this point in time and till the end of hostilities, the Americans essentially controlled the Great Lakes).

Great Britain had the largest navy in the world, but because of Niagara Falls and the rapids in the St. Lawrence River, its warships couldn't reach any of the Great Lakes. Ships to fight for control of the Great Lakes had to be built on those lakes with great difficulty. Wellington observed that the second key difficulty in achieving naval superiority was that British North America was:

...very extensive, thinly peopled, and producing but little food in proportion of their extent, ...military operations by large bodies are impracticable, unless the party carrying them on has the uninterrupted use of a navigable waterway, or very extensive means of land transport, which such a country can rarely have.

Wellington also wondered how victory could be achieved in the vast expanses of the North American land mass compounded by the problem of also having to transport men and supplies across thousands of miles of the often stormy Atlantic Ocean. The settled portion of British North America stretched over 1,300 miles from Halifax, Nova Scotia to Amherstburg in Upper Canada. To put this in perspective, this distance is only 200 miles less than that from Paris to Moscow. Further, the population of Canada was about 600,000, mostly rural and spread out, and included many French-speaking people of questionable loyalty to the British Crown. With no real manufacturing capability, all military supplies had to come from England.

In opposition were six million Americans with a fast growing industrial base. Regardless of any military or naval successes, the British might *...do no more than secure the points on those lakes at which the Americans would have access.* Most significantly, Wellington observed: *I do not know where you could carry on such an operation which would be so injurious to the Americans as to force them to sue for peace, which is what one would wish to see ...*

After Napoleon's surrender, some reinforcements became available to replace lost Indian Allies and even allow Prevost, as Bathurst would instruct him, *...to commence offensive operations on the enemy's frontier.* The goal of these attacks was apparently not, as the Americans feared, to regain the former American colonies, but to first *...give immediate protection to Canada* *secondly, to obtain if possible ultimate security to His Majesty's Possessions in America.*

By the end of 1814, the arrival in North America of a mixed bag of some Peninsular Campaign veterans supplemented by troops freed up from garrison duty in Europe, brought the overall total of troops there to over 37,000 British regulars in the northern theatre. Another 10,000 were in Maine, the Chesapeake Bay region and Louisiana, giving a grand total of 48,163 officers and men. By this time, most of the earlier 5,000 or more Indian Allies fighters had become disenchanted and gone home.

During November 1814, the Duke provided his third analysis of the American War. His military assessment remained unchanged, but his thinking now reflected Britain's fatigue and tax weariness of being at war for so long. Indeed, his own experience was a demonstration of the effects of prolonged warfare as he had been campaigning almost continuously since 1794 and had served in the peninsula without leave from 1808 to 1814. Wellington wrote, *...the continuance of the American War will entail upon us a prodigious expense, much more than we have had any idea of, along with the other burdens it would bring.*

As soon as Wellington returned from the Continent, he was offered command of all the British forces fighting in America. Wellington was not effusive over the potential appointment, but he did not, as a loyal subject and officer, shirk from it. In November 1814, Wellington informed Bathurst and Liverpool that he felt *...no objection to going to America,* but he *didn't promise to myself much success there.* His views had changed little: *...there were troops enough there for the defense of Canada ... and even for the accomplishment of any reasonable offensive plan that could be formed.* He remained confident British troops and sound generalship could prevail: *all the American armies of which I have ever read would not beat out of a field of battle the troops that went from Bordeaux last summer, if common precautions and care were taken of them.*

Wellington also noted that generalship alone would not bring the desired results: *...that which appears to me to be wanting in America is not a General, or General officers and troops, but a naval superiority on the Lakes. Till that superiority is acquired, it is impossible, according to my notion, to maintain an army in such a situation as to keep the enemy out of the whole frontier.*

It was not enough to simply send him there, Wellington wrote, and without the proper plan for securing the supply chain, he might in the end *only prove the truth of Prevost's defense.* Wellington, at this point regularly attending the Congress of Vienna, was also concerned about the unsatisfactory state of negotiations there and the alarming situation in France, which he believed made it imperative to ...*sign a peace [with the Americans] which might as well be signed now.*

This advice was accepted by the Prime Minister, who instructed the Foreign Secretary, Lord Castlereagh, that Britain should ...*not continue the war for obtaining, or securing any acquisition of territory* for the very reasons outlined by the Duke of Wellington. The plain fact was that British subjects were sick of the 20 year war with France and its costs and subsequent taxes. The politicians were looking for a way out that would still allow them to save face. It took an untouchable hero, like the Duke of Wellington, to in essence tell the government and Parliament that "their baby was ugly." He thereby provided the political cover that allowed the peace negotiators to back down on the terms to which the Americans were objecting and get the Peace Treaty signed.

Chapter VI - Three Strikes and the Peace Negotiations

"Show respect to all people, but grovel to none"
and
"Abuse no one and no thing, for abuse turns the wise ones to fools and robs the spirit of its vision"

Tecumseh

A. Effect of the Three Strikes on the Use of British Troops freed up by Defeat of Napoleon

From the beginning of the conflict through the year 1812 and most of 1813, all American attempts at invading Canada had been unsuccessful and the British attacks on American soil had primarily only been successful when they had major Indian support. In the east these few successes did not lead to permanent occupations. There were not enough Redcoats and the Indian allies would not remain for garrison duty, away from their homes.

In the west however, the British had succeeded in taking and holding several American forts, since this was a region where England and its fur traders had long term relationships with local Indians. By mid-1813, the British were in direct or indirect de-facto control of much of the area west of the Appalachians.

The Three Strikes in 1813 changed all that. By October of that year the Americans and their 15 ship fleet controlled all traffic on Lake Erie and effectively stopped the resupply and reinforcement of British installations in the west. One by one the British had to abandon their outposts. The situation was exacerbated by the death of Tecumseh. With his passing, the Indian Confederacy collapsed and the large numbers of Indian allies, upon whom the British previously had relied, were no longer there.

74

Some of the 1813 Forts and Fortified Trading Posts between the Appalachian Mountains and the Mississippi River

Ft. Mackinac – Well fortified island fortress near the junction of Lakes Huron, Michigan and Superior. The British were able to capture and sustain this stronghold through the war only because it could be supplied overland from the Burlington Heights base on Lake Ontario over the old fur trading route to NW Lake Huron.

Ft. Shelby (later British Ft McKay) - Protected the village of Prairie du Chen, Wisconsin and former French fur trading center

Ft Osage (near present day Kansas City, Missouri) Largest fur trading post in region

Ft Madison (Iowa) - First fort in the area & second largest fur trading post. Site of only battle of the War of 1812 fought west of the Mississippi River

Ft Belle Fontaine - (near present day St. Louis, Missouri) Hqtrs. of US Army in the upper Mississippi area

Ft Johnson – (near present day Warsaw, Illinois)

Ft Cap Au Gris – (near present day Troy, Missouri)

Ft. Dearborn – (near present day Chicago, Illinois)

The principal good news that Britain had, in late 1813 and early 1814, was that Napoleon had been defeated and negotiations were underway that ultimately led to his abdication. This freed up British regulars, who had been fighting Napoleon or manning European garrisons, for duty in Canada replacing the lost Indian warriors. However, by this time, thanks to a large extent to the Three Strikes, the British situation in Canada had radically changed. These changes reduced the range of choices Britain had available to utilize these newly available troops.

The Americans, with their large fleet, were in control of Lake Erie and access to the rest of the Upper Lakes. They also had enough of a fleet on Lake Ontario that it was no longer possible to stage attacks from this area with impunity. As noted previously, when the Duke of Wellington was offered command of the American theatre at this point, he told the British Government that, unless they could guarantee him naval mastery of all the Great Lakes, even he probably could not do them any good.

A side benefit to the Americans was that, with the British in the west gone and the Indian Confederacy broken, western troops and militia were freed up to shore up the vulnerable places in the east. In essence, the British could only use the new troops to mount attacks from the small portions of Canada east of Montreal or raid American cities on the Atlantic and Gulf coast. Using them for long term occupation, of any portion of the American coastal States not contiguous to Canada, was infeasible. Given these constaints, the British chose a new, four-prong strategy.

For the first prong, they launched a major invasion with over 10,000 veteran Redcoats supported by a small flotilla of ships, down Lake Champlain. The ultimate intent was to drive south, down the Hudson River, to New York, effectively splitting the US. The American Lake Champlain fleet was waiting for them in Plattsburgh and the Americans were victorious in a most unusual naval battle. It was unusual in that the bay, where the battle took place, was so confined that most of the ships on both sides were at anchor as they fought. It was to some degree an artillery engagement from floating batteries rather than a true naval battle. Reluctant to proceed without the military and logistical support of a fleet, the British marched back to Montreal.

A small, second attack on what is now northern Maine[9] managed to occupy the lightly-populated northeast corner as far south as Bangor. This was a minor affair to the Americans but important to the British since they wanted to secure a shorter route between Montreal and Halifax. (The Maine border line had been in dispute for years.)

The third prong in these assaults was the raid that seized and burned ill prepared and poorly defended Washington. This was a psychological blow to the US but had little military significance. This same British force then proceeded to Baltimore with the intent of destroying this important port and its shipping. A large number of the privateers, that were plaguing British shipping, were based here. The Americans were far better prepared at Baltimore. Despite heavy shelling by the substantial number of major warships the British had in their invasion fleet, Fort McHenry and the other defenses protecting Baltimore held and the British had to sail away empty handed..

The fourth prong of the assault with the new, battle hardened regulars was aimed at capturing the port of New Orleans. Because they had to wait until the storm season in the Gulf had passed, by the time this fleet reached New Orleans and staged their attack, the Peace Treaty already had been signed. Unfortunately, communication was slow in these days so neither side knew that the war was effectively over. The poorly planned main British attack took place across unfamiliar ground in a heavy fog against a strong and well dug-in, large American force. It was a major military disaster for the British.

---

[9] This area was part of Massachusetts at this time.

B. The Effect of Three Strikes and the Congress of Vienna on the Peace Negotiations

The British and Americans met at Ghent, Belgium to begin peace negotiations. The initial negotiations got underway on a very antagonistic basis. It turned out that, unknown to the Congress, England already had repealed the more onerous laws affecting trade just weeks before the U. S. declared war. With the war in Europe winding down, so was the urgent need for seamen that had sparked impressment. Therefore, two of the original issues were now somewhat moot.

The remaining stumbling block, therefore, was that the British, in honoring the treaties they had signed with their Indian allies, demanded a large block of the United States be set aside as an Indian homeland. They also wanted this entity strategically to serve as a buffer between the U. S. and the Canadian provinces. The British started off the meeting by telling the US negotiators that this Indian homeland position was not subject to negotiation.

Gallatin, one of the US negotiators, wrote to his son that the British demanded that the

Indian tribes should have the whole of the North-Western Territory. This comprises the States of Michigan, Wisconsin, and Illinois—four fifths of Indiana and a third of Ohio. That an Indian sovereignty should be constituted under the guarantee of Great Britain: this is to protect Canada... But all this means is the dismemberment of the United States.

It must be borne in mind that, in August of 1814 when the negotiators first met, the British, the Canadians and their remaining Indian allies were still riding high with a good record of military successes, at least on land. They had even burned Washington, DC. Napoleon had just abdicated and the British no doubt felt that, with large number of veteran troops now available, the war could be brought to a swift conclusion. The British no doubt felt that they could pretty well dictate terms.

The Americans knew that the President, Congress and the American people would never accede to carving out an Indian homeland. Thanks to the Three Strikes, they could point out that the U. S. controlled most of the Great Lakes and the area west of the mountains being referred to as "Quebec" or "Indian Homeland". They could point out that England's ally, Tecumseh's Indian Confederation, many of whose members lived in this region, had been scattered as a broken and dispersed force.

It looked like an impasse was a possibility. And then several things happened.

First, as noted above and partly because the Three Strikes had limited British options, the four-pronged attack with all the fresh troops did not come up to expectations. The attacks on Lake Champlain and Baltimore were defeated. The attack on what is now Maine yielded a few hundred square miles of forest and a shortcut to Halifax and not much else. The planned attack on New Orleans was delayed, waiting for the end of the storm season.

Second, the Congress of Vienna commanded the attentions of Europe. At this meeting, the senior diplomats of the conquering nations and of defeated France sat down to essentially redraw the map of Europe in an attempt to create conditions for an enduring peace. This was the big deal of diplomacy and all the top diplomats were in attendance.

By comparison, the negotiations at Ghent were a side show. Viscount Castlereagh, England's Secretary for Foreign Affairs and one time Leader of the House of Commons, to whom the British team at Ghent reported, would stop by and give the team guidance on his way to and from Vienna Congress meetings.

Castlereagh headed up the English delegation at Vienna which included the Duke of Wellington, the victor at Waterloo. Castlereagh and his team were attempting to restrain the more aggressive territorial demands of Prussia and Russia and other points of disagreement. In trying to take the high moral ground with its allies in the Napoleonic War and get agreement on decisions most likely to maintain the peace in Europe, the fact England was still embroiled in what appeared to be a no-win contest with its former colonies, was an embarrassment to England.

Another factor influencing Castlereagh was that, as at one point having been Leader of the House of Commons, he knew that members of Parliament, responding to input from constituents, were becoming increasingly opposed to continuing the war with America and the expense thereof. It seemed like, each time he visited Ghent, he gave permission for the negotiators to back off further from the original rigid position regarding the Indians.

As mentioned earlier, the British leaders also got a dose of military common sense from the Duke of Wellington. He was offered command of the British forces in the American war. His advice was: *I think that you might as well sign a peace treaty with the United States now. I think you have no right to demand any territory from the United States. The failure of the British military campaigns in America gives you no right to make such demands.* In the end, England backed off on the Indian issue. The result was a Treaty with very innocuous, feel-good language palatable to the Americans which guaranteed little to the Indians.

C. Effect of Losing the Three Strikes on European History

Had America not prevailed in the Three Strikes on the Upper Lakes (and assuming the British could then have destroyed or at least bottled up the remaining American fleet on Lake Ontario) Wellington's criteria for success, control of the Great Lakes, would have been met. If Wellington, arguably one of the most skilled Generals in the world at the time, would then have come to America backed with, say, 50,000 of his well equipped, veteran troops, thousands of still available Indian Confederacy warriors and an assured supply line, the U.S. might have ultimately been forced to accept a treaty with substantial territorial losses.

Remember though, Napoleon came out of exile in early 1815 and remobilized the French Army. Wellington and the cream of the British Army might still have been off fighting in the North American wilderness. It would have taken months to disengage them and get them back to Europe. Therefore, when Generalfeldmarschall von Blücher and his Prussian Army arrived at Waterloo there might have been no Wellington and his British Army waiting to join him in taking on Napoleon and the French Army. Without the British, the Prussians and the small, allied contingents from Holland and several German States would have been outnumbered and Napoleon might well have prevailed. So European as well as American history might have been indirectly but drastically changed if not for America's success at the Three Strikes.

Chapter VII – Postwar U. S. and British Relations

A -Tying up a Loose End

Although the War of 1812 ended on February 17, 1815 the border details were not finalized until 1822. The Treaty specified that, where the border between the US and Canada was a body of water, the border followed the deepest point. The Niagara River flows around both sides of Grand Island. When surveyed, it was found that the channel between the island and the Canadian shore, was deeper than the eastern channel between the island and the American shore. Grand Island became part of the US.

B – The later years

No one could have predicted it at the time, but when the Treaty of Ghent was ratified, it marked the last time the US and England faced off as foes. In the earlier years of this period, however, there was still a lot of distrust. Great Britain and Canada moved the capital of Canada to Ottawa, further from the US border and dug the Rideau Canal to bypass the St. Lawrence River. They feared the US might seize control of the St. Lawrence and block the flow of supplies to Ottawa and Lake Ontario in wartime.

Although the Treaty called for a very limited naval presence on the Upper Lakes, the British flaunted this restriction. The U.S. therefore decided to build, in Erie, Pennsylvania the *USS Michigan,* the US Navy's first iron, steam-powered warship. Since very large rolling mills were needed to shape the iron plates to the curvature of the hull and there were none sizable enough in Erie, the plates were rolled in Pittsburgh and the whole hull bolted together there to make sure everything fitted. Thereafter, the hull was taken apart and shipped via the newly-opened canals that linked the Ohio River to Lake Erie. The hull was then riveted together in Erie.

Reportedly one of the fastest warships in the world at the time and continually updated with the most modern armament, the *Michigan* alone restored the US's military dominance on the Lakes. Launched in 1843, she continued to enforce the law on the Upper Lakes in various capacities until she was decommissioned in 1912. She was one of the longest serving ships in the US Navy.

The Civil War era marked the midpoint of the American/British transition from foe to ally. The Confederate States hoped to bring England in on their side. They assumed that England's flagship textile industry would be so affected by the Union's cutoff of cotton shipments that Great Britain would intervene. The English did go so far as sending military observers to travel with the Confederate Army. Between the reports coming back from the observers and the new availability of Egyptian cotton, England decided not to get involved.

Chapter VIII – Long Range Strategic Consequences

"Love your life, perfect your life, beautify all things in your life"
and
"Seek to make your life long and of service to your people
Tecumseh

As noted in Chapter I, an interrelated series of three major, 1813 American victories (plus a battle that never was) probably had a profound impact on the territorial outcome of that war. This outcome, in turn, had a profound impact on the subsequent history and fortunes of the United States. There were two net strategic results of these three victories.

A - Britain

First, by late 1813, thanks to the capture of the entire British squadron, the United States and its new, large fleet controlled all traffic on the upper lakes for the rest of the war. Therefore the British held forts and outposts in the northern Mississippi River basin could no longer be supplied and supported and eventually had to be abandoned.

As noted previously, just before the American Revolution, Parliament passed the Quebec Act of 1774 which would have made much of the territory described above part of the Province of Quebec. After the Revolutionary War, the British had continued to look for a way to return this territory to Canada.

Peace negotiations between the United States and Great Britain began in 1814. If the British had been in possession of this portion of the Midwest during the negotiations, they might very well have been able to insist (per the international law concept of *uti possidetis* on keeping this area as part of Canada.

B – Indian Confederation

If the close alliance between the Crown and the Indian Confederation, and to some degree among the members of the Confederation itself, had not both been broken by the Three Strike victories, the Indian Confederation probably would have had to be given a seat at the table at the Peace Conference. The Indian Confederation would have been able to carve out, as part of the peace treaty, some territory/country of their own, per the Crown's commitments to them. The US might then have been limited in its westward expansion. In the north an expanded Quebec would be blocking the Mid-Atlantic States' westward access. The land west of Georgia, the Carolinas and Virginia (and portions of southern Illinois and Indiana) would be under Indian control and the ability to develop the Louisiana Purchase lands west of the Mississippi River would have been severely hampered.

The breaking of the alliance between Britain and the Indian Confederation and the British inability to support the tribes with material and military helped removed much of the restraints on America's westward expansion. The settlers were able (largely unchecked) to force the Indians to abandon their historic lands and be pushed further west or on to reservations. The US felt free to abrogate prewar treaties and "open up" former tribal lands to settlers. It was no coincidence that the ink was barely dry on the Treaty of Ghent when four new States were created from these lands in a three year period (Indiana 1816, Mississippi 1817, Illinois 1818 and Alabama 1819)

C - If England had gained the U.S. West of the Appalachians

First, let us flash forward to the Mexican American War. If the British and the Indian Nation Confederacy were in possession of all of North America between the Appalachian Mountains and the Mississippi, Texas would have been the only territory next to the (probably under populated) Louisiana Purchase lands. The much shrunken US might not have gotten involved in a war

If we now roll our history forward to the Civil War, the consequences of a British victory could have been a real history changer. If what became the States of Michigan, Minnesota, Wisconsin, Indiana and Illinois were still part of Quebec, Canada, when the Civil War broke out, the North would had far less troops and resources for the war effort. On the other hand, if the Indian Confederation Nation had survived as an entity for the intervening years, what are now the States of Alabama and Mississippi might have still been under Indian control and never have become part of the Confederate States at all.

The Civil War therefore could have been fought largely between the eighteen states that existed when the War of 1812 ended, with a hard-to-predict outcome.

Appendix A -Chronology of Events Covered

October 9, 1812 – The *Caledonia* is captured at Fort Erie by Americans. (*Caledonia* would be critical success factor in Battle of Lake Erie)

April 27, 1813 – An American amphibious raid captures armament destined for the *Detroit* (flagship of the British Lake Erie fleet) being built in Amherstburg. Loss of these armaments would be a critical success factor in Battle of Lake Erie and (indirectly) the Battle of Moraviantown.

May 27, 1813 – The Americans take Fort George, forcing the British to evacuate Fort Erie and providing Perry an opportunity to bring the *Caledonia*, the *Trippe*, the *Sommers*, the *Amelia* and the *Ohio* down from Black Rock (Buffalo) to join his fleet in Erie.

September 10, 1813 - At the Battle of Lake Erie, the Americans defeat and capture the entire British fleet.

October 5, 1813 – At the Battle of Moraviantown,
Tecumseh is killed. The Indian Confederacy disintegrates.

May 1814 – Napoleon abdicates, freeing up British troops to replace the loss of Indian Allies fighters.

August 1814 – Peace negotiations begin in Ghent.

August 24, 1815 – Washington, DC is captured and burned.

September 11, 1814 – At the Battle of Plattsburgh (Battle of Lake Champlain) the British are defeated and retreat back to Canada. The planned Montreal to New York invasion is averted.

September 13-14, 1814 – The British assault to destroy the Port of Baltimore is checked at Fort McHenry.

September 1815 – British occupy northeastern Maine (to Bangor).

September 1814 – The Congress of Vienna convenes and Europe is restructured by the victors and the vanquished.

December 24, 1814 – Ghent Peace Treaty is signed.

January 8, 1815 – At the ante bellum Battle of New Orleans, British are decisively defeated.

February 16, 1815 – The U. S. Senate ratifies the Peace Treaty.

March 1815 – Napoleon flees exile and reclaims his throne.

June 1815 – Napoleon's army is defeated at Waterloo and he goes into final exile.

Appendix B – Cannon Facts and Specifications

1 - Naval cannon

The "24-pounder" long gun was muzzle-loading, long-barreled cannon capable of firing a solid iron shot weighing 24 pounds. Mounted on a four-wheel carriage, it had a maximum effective range of about 1,200 yards (2/3 of a mile) and could be fired about once every three minutes by a trained crew of twelve men and a boy (the "powder monkey"). The "Furnace Hope Model" was 8 feet long and had a bore of about 5 5/6". When on its carriage, this 24-pounder long gun weighed about 6,000 pounds.

Each 18-pounder long gun weighed on the order of 4,700 pounds and was 8 feet long. Each 12-pounder was about the same length but weighed about 4,100 pounds. Their crews were proportionately somewhat smaller than those for the 24 pounders, but the firing rates were similar.

A "carronade" was a short-barreled, large bore, relatively lightweight muzzle-loading weapon of murderous short-range (400 yards maximum effective) smashing power. The 32-pounder version was only 4 feet long and weighed about 2000 pounds. It required a smaller gun crew and, because of its lightness, could be mounted in larger numbers and higher in the ship than long guns. Unlike the long gun, it was mounted on a slanted slide bed that absorbed the recoil energy by lifting the weight of the carronade as it slid back. It was also pivoted to allow it to be aimed in an arc.

2 – Cannon materials

Most British and American naval cannon of the 1812 period were cast from iron. Each unit was solid cast iron bored out to the specified diameter. The advantages of cast iron were that it was relatively inexpensive, strong and could be cast in large shapes. One of the disadvantages of cast iron for naval use, particularly in the salty oceans, was that it rusted readily and the rust continually sloughed off. To slow this effect, iron cannon have to be painted regularly and the barrel oiled and sealed when not in use. Another disadvantage is that it is brittle. When a cast iron cannon explodes during a battle due to, say, overloading, it shatters, scattering shrapnel all around. This is why the armies used bronze (*see* below) for cannon advancing amidst the infantry.

The Spaniards had better access to copper and tin, particularly once the South American mines were discovered. They therefore tended to make their naval cannon out of bronze. Bronze has the advantage that any corrosion forms an adhering layer, the patina, which protects the metal underneath. A second advantage of bronze, particularly when being used in close proximity to large numbers of men (like advancing infantry or in an amphibious operation) is that usually, when the cannon barrel fails, it tends to split rather than splinter into shrapnel.

The British 3-pounder (nicknamed the "Grasshopper") commonly imbedded with infantry (rather than used in batteries) was made of bronze. This gun was small and light enough that the crew could roll it along themselves for a fair distance in a march or in a battle. It did not always require the complication of being hitched to a team of horses each time, like the heavier artillery.

Some small cannon, up to 3-pounders, could be fitted with yokes equipped with a pin that fitted into holes in the ships railings like those holes provided for belaying pins used for securing lines. On ships the small, rail mounted cannon were commonly used for clearing the decks of opposing warship's crew when the ships got into close proximity. These cannon also could be mounted in the bow of the longboats to sweep the beach of any defenders. Cannons above 3-pounders were not typically used rail mounted because, when fired, the recoil put too much strain on the railing. Cannon larger than 3 pounder were also were too heavy for easy lifting on to the rail

3 – Gun Handling

In the 50 years of almost continual naval warfare leading up to 1812, advances in metallurgy and carriage design resulted in lighter armaments, but the weight of smoothbore artillery was still considerable. The standard British light 6-pounder, complete with carriage, weighed around 1,700 pounds while an American 6-pounder gun with carriage weighed 2,000 pounds and an American 12-pounder gun with carriage about 2,900 pounds. On firing, these weapons recoiled from four to six feet and had to be "run up" or returned to their firing position by brute strength before the next round was fired. Gunners of the War of 1812 had to be big, strong men. In the Royal Artillery, for instance, recruits were required to weigh a minimum of 182 pounds.

During the War of 1812, a dedicated British gun team consisted of 5 numbered gunners - smaller crews than needed in the previous century. The No. 1 was the gun commander, a sergeant, who aimed the gun. The No. 2 was the "spongeman" who cleaned the bore with a sponge dampened with water between shots; the intention being to quench any remaining embers before a fresh charge was introduced. The No. 3, the loader, inserted the bag of powder and then the projectile. The No. 2 then used a rammer, or the sponge reversed, to drive them in. At the same time, the No. 4 ("ventsman") pressed his thumb on the vent hole to prevent a draught that might fan a flame. The charge loaded, the No. 4 pricked the bagged charge through the vent hole and filled the vent with powder. No. 1's aimed down the barrel and, when the target lined up, pulled the firing cord tied to the gunlock mechanism. If no gunlock was available, Number 1 would aim and then give the "Fire" command. No. 5 would fire the piece with his linstock (or slowmatch). In addition to the dedicated gun team, there was a boy to bring up ammunition. After loading, it took five or more additional soldiers, seamen or marines, in addition to the gun crew, to help wrestle the gun back into firing position.

4 – The Physics of Gunnery

In the 1812 era it was estimated that a 24- pounder could fire 90 to 100 shots a day in summer, or 60 to 75 in winter. A 16 or 12-pounder would fire a little faster, because they were more easily served. *The Encyclopedia Britannica* cites some instances where it was reported that 200 shots have been fired from these pieces in the space of nine hours (2.7 minutes between firings), and, on another occasion, 138 shots in the space of five hours.(2.2 minutes between firing)

The most important advantage of heavy cannon balls is this, that with the same velocity they break larger holes out in all solid bodies. For instance, a twenty-four pound shot will, with the same velocity, break out a hole in any wall or solid beam, in which it lodges, above eight times larger than will be made by a three pound shot. Since its diameter is double, it will make a superficial fracture above four times as great as the three-pounder ball.

More of a smaller hole is typically closed up by the spring back of the solid wood body than of a large hole. The heavier shot will also penetrate to more than twice the depth. In ships the strongest beams, bulwarks and masts are readily fractured, which great numbers of small cannon balls would scarcely injure.

A 24-pounder cannon, with the normal six pound gunpowder charge, would have a muzzle velocity of 770 mph and an extreme range of 1.1 mile. About ¾ of a mile range is probably more realistic in most cases.

5 – Pivot Mounts

Cannon on ships in the Revolutionary War era traditionally were mounted in rows for the broadside to broadside type of naval warfare. The War of 1812 saw the introduction of cannon mounted on pivoting bases that allowed them to be aimed and fired over a range of angles relative to the ship's direction of sailing. A number of Perry's smaller ships, like the *Caledonia* and the *Scorpion* were equipped with swivel-mounted long guns which allowed them to fire on the *Detroit* and the *Queen Charlotte* from an angle that did not expose themselves to those British ship's broadside-facing cannon. The pivot mount eventually evolved into today's turrets.

6 - A little piece of "cannon trivia".

The brass monkey, in reference to quantifying how cold it is, actually has nothing to do with primates (metal or otherwise) or their genitals. Its origin is nautical.

It was desirable to store cannonballs on deck near the cannon so that they would be immediately at hand when needed. It would be a problem to keep them from rolling around the deck as the ship moved. The solution was to stack them up in a square-based pyramid next to the cannon. To keep the bottom level from sliding out from under the weight of the higher levels, a small brass plate, called a, brass monkey, with one rounded indentation for each cannonball in the bottom layer, was devised. Brass was used so the iron cannonballs would not rust to the brass plate.

However, brass contracts to a much greater degree than iron when the temperature falls, so when it got extremely cold on the gun decks, the indentations, and their spacing on the brass monkey, would get smaller than spacing of the iron cannonballs they were holding. Conceivably, if it got really cold enough, the bottom layer of cannon balls could pop out of the indentations, spilling the entire pyramid over the deck. Thus it was, quite literally, cold enough to freeze the balls off a brass monkey.

APPENDIX C - Gunlocks

A gunlock was a flintlock mechanism for firing a cannon. First used by the Royal Navy in 1745, they were a significant innovation in naval gunnery. Their use spread slowly as they could not easily be retrofitted to older guns.

Prior to the introduction of the gunlock, the method of firing a cannon was to apply a linstock - a wooden staff with a length of smoldering match at the end - to the touch-hole of the gun filled with loose priming powder. As the gun had to be fired from the side, to avoid its recoil, this was dangerous and made accurate shooting from a moving ship impossible. Also, there was a noticeable (and variable) delay between the order fire (apply the linstock/slowmatch) and the gun actually firing.

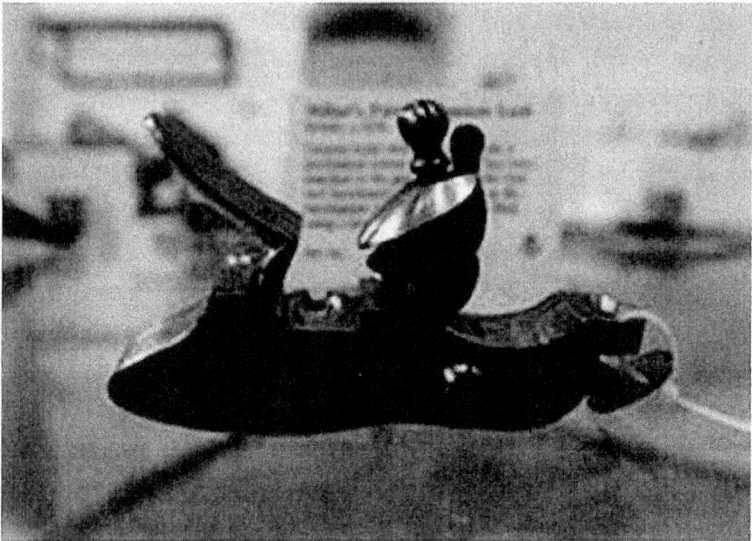

"Cannon lock 1820" by geni - Photo by user:geni. Licensed under GFDL via Wikimedia

By comparison, the gunlock was operated by pulling a cord, or lanyard. Loading the gun was faster and safer because the gunlock did not use loose priming powder; the main charge was ignited by a quill filled with priming powder that was pushed through the touch hole during loading and pierced the cartridge bag containing the main charge of gunpowder. More importantly, the gun-captain could stand behind the gun, safely beyond its range of recoil, and sight along the gun, firing precisely by pulling the cord from ther gunlock when the roll of the ship lined the gun up with the enemy vessel.

Because fortress guns were used in fixed target land installations, none of these required gunlocks. When Barclay stripped the western forts of cannon for the *Detroit*, these so called "fortress cannon" probably lacked these state-of-the-art gunlock firing mechanisms. As noted previously, the gunlocks intended for the *Detroit* had been seized by the Americans. None were found aboard the *Detroit* when she was captured.

Appendix D – Tecumseh

1. Seeds of the Indian Confederacy of 1812

The territorial provisions in the1795 Treaty of Greenville meant that many tribes had to move off their traditional hunting grounds and shift further west. The Miami tribe invited the ejected Lenape and Shawnee tribes to settle in land in what is Ohio and Indiana but, at the time, was considered part of Miami holdings. The Shawnee moved into northwestern Ohio and Northeastern Indiana and the Lenape moved into parts of south-central Indiana.

The tribes increasingly intermingled one with the other and most villages contained inhabitants of multiple tribes. Leadership became increasingly organized at the village rather than tribal level, so in most cases, a leader represented members of multiple tribes who were living together in the same settlement as several tribes came to live in the same geographic area.

2. Religious revival

In May 1805, the leader of the Lenape Tribe, Chief Buckongahelas, one of the most important native leaders in the region, but also one who believed in co-existence with the settlers, died suddenly.. The word somehow spread that his death was caused by a form of witchcraft, and a widespread witch hunt ensued leading to the death of several suspected Lenape witches.

A young Shawnee leader named Tenskwatawa saw the opportunity and seized upon this spontaneous burst of religious fervor. He succeeded in molding it into a unifying religious movement that brought a number of tribes together in a common cause.. Tenskwatawa was influenced greatly by the teachings of several former Lenape religious leaders who had predicted a coming apocalypse in which the white men would be overthrown by supernatural powers. As part of Tenskwatawa's religious teachings, he urged Indians to reject the ways of the whites, like liquor, Europeans style clothing, and even firearms. He also called for the tribes to refrain from ceding any more lands to the States

His growing influence quickly posed a threat to the authority of all the local chiefs. These other tribal leaders put pressure on Tenskwatawa and his followers to leave the area to prevent the situation from perhaps escalating into an open conflict with the settlers

The Pottawatomie Chief, Winamac, who was also a religious leader calling for a return to many of the old ways offered them sanctuary. (This Chief, however, was a one of the strongest voices in urging the Indians to adapt the agricultural methods of the settlers). Tenskwatawa accepted the invitation and established the village (called Prophetstown by the settlers) very near the confluence of the Wabash and Tippecanoe Rivers.

Tenskwatawa's religious teachings became increasingly militant following a 1807 treaty that forced Fox and Sauk tribes off much of their land. Many members of the two tribes were angered by the treaty. The Piankeshaw and Kickapoo also had been adversely affected by other treaties and migrated closer to Prophetstown. His growing popularity attracted Native American followers from many different tribes, including the Iroquois, Chickamauga, Ojibway and Mascouten.

Prophetstown (aka Tippecanoe) was not only the largest Native American community in the Great Lakes region but served as a major center of Indian culture and a deterrent against settler incursions. It became an intertribal, religious stronghold for three thousand Native Americans. Led by Tenskwatawa (by now nicknamed "The Prophet") thousands of these Algonquin-speaking Indians gathered at Tippecanoe to gain spiritual strength (and perhaps receive some training in up-to-date warfare skills).

3. The Rise of Tecumseh

By 1808, Tecumseh, Tenskwatawa's older brother, began to be seen as a rising political and military leader by his community. He was outraged by the continued loss of land to the whites and he began to travel around the Great Lakes region to visit village leaders and urge them to stop cooperating with the settlers and threatening to kill chiefs who continued to work with them. His goal was to create a pan-tribal confederacy powerful enough to counter and resist the United States. His travels triggered the largest growth yet in the Confederacy as numerous villages agreed to join in his resistance. Even villages which did not totally accept Tecumseh's argument had some individuals who would leave and move to Prophetstown, continuing to swell his numbers.

Although he ultimately emerged as the leader of the Confederation, the movement was built upon a foundation established by the religious zeal and appeal of his younger brother. At the height of his influence, Tecumseh was said to have more than 5,000 warriors under his leadership,. In late 1808, the British, seeing an opportunity, approached Tecumseh to form an alliance. He declined.

In 1811, he traveled south to meet with leaders of the Five Civilized Tribes to try to get them to join the Confederacy. He had a vision of an Indian Nation that would be powerful enough to hold all the lands west of the Appalachian Mountains. The chiefs of the tribes in the South were, at the time, still leaned toward having a peaceable relationship with the settlers. Tecumseh was met with resistance and rejection and returned north. Only a group from one southern tribes, the Creeks, joined his Confederacy

4. Tecumseh's War

Tensions already had been rising rapidly as the Americans had become aware of Tecumseh's war aims. While he was still in the

South with many of his warriors, a preemptive strike was launched against Prophetstown, defeating his brother and a force of 500–700 warriors in the much touted Battle of Tippecanoe..

Tecumseh returned and began to rebuild. He met and formed a "brothers in arms" relationship with the new and very capable British commander, General Brock. Brock convinced him of the sincerity of the British proposals and he, on behalf of the Indian Confederation, entered into a British alliance at the outbreak of the War of 1812, Tecumseh began a series of coordinated raids on American posts in Indian dominated territories. The Americans responded and launched a second campaign, destroying Prophetstown a second time. Tecumseh's frontier war forced the Americans into a defensive posture, which divided their forces and probably helped prevent the Americans from concentrating large enough of troops to successfully invade and occupy the strategically important area of Lower Canada (current Quebec).

Appendix E   Tecumseh's Letter to General Procter

FATHER, listen to your children! You have them now all before you. The war before this, our British father gave the hatchet to his red children when old chiefs were alive. They are now dead. In that war our father was thrown on his back by the Americans, and our father took them by the hand without our knowledge; and we are afraid that our father will do so again at this time.

Summer before last, when I came forward with my red brethren and was ready to take up the hatchet in favor of our British father, we were told not to be in a hurry; that he had not yet determined to fight the Americans.

Listen! When war was declared, our father stood up and gave us the tomahawk, and told us that he was ready to strike the Americans; that he wanted our assistance, and that he would certainly get us our lands back, which the Americans had taken from us.

Listen! You told us at that time to bring forward our families to this place, and we did so; and you promised to take care of them, and that they should want for nothing while the men would go and fight the enemy. That we need not trouble ourselves about the enemy's garrisons; that we knew nothing about them, and that our father would attend to that part of the business. You also told your red children that you would take good care of your garrison here, which made our hearts glad.

Listen! When we were last at the Rapids, it is true we gave you little assistance. It is hard to fight people who live like ground-hogs.

Father, listen! Our fleet has gone out; we know they have fought; we have heard the great guns, but know nothing of what has happened to our father with one arm. Our ships have gone one way, and we are much astonished to see our father tying up everything and preparing to run away the other, without letting his red children know what his intentions are. You always told us to remain here and take care of our lands. It made our hearts glad to hear that was your wish. Our great father, the king, is the head, and you represent him. You always told us that you would never draw your foot off British ground; but now, father, we see you are drawing back, and we are sorry to see our father doing so without seeing the enemy. We must compare our father's conduct to a fat animal that carries its tail upon its back, but when affrighted it drops it between its legs and runs off.

Listen, father! The Americans have not yet defeated us by land; neither are we sure that they have done so by water; we therefore wish to remain here and fight our enemy should they make their appearance. If they defeat us, we will then retreat with our father.

At the Battle of the Rapids, last war, the Americans certainly defeated us; and when we retreated to our fathers fort in that place the gates were shut against us. We were afraid that it would now be the case, but instead of that we now see our British father preparing to march out of his garrison.

Father! You have got the arms and ammunition which our great father sent for his red children. If you have an idea of going away, give them to us, and you may go and welcome; for us, our lives are in the hands of the Great Spirit. We are determined to defend our lands, and if it is His will we wish to leave our bones upon them.

Appendix F - The Career of Usher Parsons

In this book Usher is cited for the remarkable results he achieved, under the most difficult medical conditions imaginable, at the Battle of Lake Erie. Usher Parsons went on to have a most distinguished career.

His career had started modestly. After studying under physicians in Maine and in Boston, Parsons managed to secure a commission as a Naval Surgeon's Mate at the outset of the war of 1812. In today's navy, this might be considered the equivalent to being a Hospital Corpsman. He was assigned to the fleet being assembled at Erie, Pennsylvania under the command of Commodore Perry.

When both Naval Surgeons assigned to the *Lawrence* were so weak with dysentery that they could not function, Parsons stepped in and became the senior medical person aboard. During the battle, the *Lawrence* suffered what remains one of the record high percentages of casualties in naval history, with 80% of the crew either killed or wounded. As noted earlier, during the battle and extending to the day after, Parsons performed about 100 surgeries, with an unprecedented, to that point in history, 96% survival rate. This record stood until WWI. After the war, Parsons remained under Perry's command, serving on the frigate

Java, which sailed to Algiers and other Mediterranean ports, returning in March 1817.

Parsons finally obtained his official medical degree, at Harvard. After his discharge from the Navy, Parsons settled permanently in Providence, Rhode Island. He married Mary Jackson Holmes (1802-1825), the sister of famed poet Oliver Wendell Holmes. By an amazing coincidence, it was Oliver Wendell Holmes who, while he was at Harvard in 1842, recommended that physicians wash their hands with a calcium chloride solution to prevent the spread of infection from the autopsy rooms to the wards.

Parsons was a professor of anatomy and surgery at Brown University from 1823 to 1828. He went on to be President of the Rhode Island Medical Society from 1837 to 1839 and in 1853 served as acting president of the American Medical Association.

Usher turned out to be somewhat of a "Renaissance Man" with a number of interests outside of medicine. He was the founding president of the Rhode Island Natural History Society and active in its early years. He combined two of his interests when he authored *A Brief Account of the Early Physicians and of the Medical Society of Rhode Island* as well as numerous other medical and historical articles and addresses. He also was a lifetime avid genealogist.

Although Parsons went on to have this very distinguished later career, he has never been given the recognition he deserves for being one of the true pioneers in surgery sterilization practices for his actions at the Battle of Lake Erie.

Appendix G - The Flip Side of Victory

Each of the three American victories meant a corresponding British defeat. The three British commanders in each instance fared quite differently.

1. The Battle of York

General Sheaffe, the Lieutenant Governor of Upper Canada, was in York just passing through en route to with some British reinforcements for other bases when the Americans attacked York. He assumed command of the defense. When he saw that the Americans, supported by ships providing covering fire, were overwhelming the defenses, he withdrew all the British regular troops and retreated back to the main British base at Kingston. In departing, he advised the townspeople, the militia and their Ojibwa Indian allies to make whatever terms they could with the victorious Americans.

Many members of the Provincial Assembly and other prominent York citizens severely criticized Sheaffe, both for leaving them at the mercy of the Americans and his conduct generally during the fighting at York. For example, Militia officers Chewitt and Allan, the Reverend Strachan (who had to negotiate with the American officers) and others wrote to Governor General Prevost in May, that Sheaffe ...*kept too far from his troops after retreating from the woods, never cheered or animated them, nor showed by his personal conduct that he was hearty in the cause.* The Governor, Sir George Prevost, relieved Sheaffe of his military and civil appointments in Upper Canada, putting him in charge of Montreal's troops (away from the action).

Two things probably shielded Sheaffe from more serious punishment. First, he had previously been awarded a baronetcy for his role as successor in command when General Brock died at the Battle of Queenston Heights. (Although not a peer, a baronet is still a member of the gentry, ranking above a Knightage).

Second, though he was perceived as treating the people of York harshly, most British senior officers felt that, by preserving the very short supply of regular British troops and not risking them on a lost cause, Sheaffe had made a defensible decision.

Later in the year, Sheaffe was recalled to Britain. Here he subsequently had a successful military career, being promoted to Lieutenant-General in 1821 and full General in 1835.

2. The Battle of Lake Erie

Commodore Barclay was brought up before a court-martial for the loss of the entire British fleet at the Battle of Lake Erie. The Court took into account the serious handicaps with which he had to go into battle. He was exonerated of any blame. He remained in the Royal Navy but it was several years before he could return to active duty due to his serious wounds.

3. The Battle of Moraviantown

General Procter, who led the retreat from Amherstburg and the Battle of Moraviantown, received the most serious repercussions. In May 1814, Procter was charged with negligence and improper conduct. The court martial could not be held until December, when campaigning had ceased for the winter and a suitably senior board of officers could be assembled. The court judged that Procter had managed the retreat badly, failed to secure his stores, and also disposed the troops ineffectively at Moraviantown. He was sentenced to be suspended from rank and pay for six months.

Appendix H -The Case of Lt. Elliot

Lt. Jesse Elliot was the Captain of the brig *Niagara* which, together with the identical *Lawrence* were the two largest ships in the American fleet at the Battle of Lake Erie. Commodore Oliver Hazard Perry, on the *Lawrence*, was the Commander of the entire squadron of nine ships (a role Elliot felt should have been his).

The American line of battle led off with two schooners, the *Ariel* and the *Scorpion*, both equipped with a small number of cannon but of a type capable of engaging the British at long range. Next came the *Lawrence*, primarily armed with very large caliber, but short range, carronades. This ship had to brave fire from the long guns of the main British ship, the corvette *Detroit*, until it got into carronade range where it and the *Detroit* could exchange broadsides. Following the *Lawrence* in line was the small, 3 gun brig *Caledonia*. The *Niagara* was supposed to be then next in line but instead reportedly hung back (by some accounts ½ a mile).

The second largest British ship, the *Queen Charlotte*, was originally positioned in the British line so as to engage the *Niagara*. However, seeing that his expected opponent was still somewhat far off, the Queen Charlotte's Captain had his ship move up the line and join the *Detroit* in pounding the *Lawrence*. During the same time the American gunboats *Caledonia*, *Ariel* and *Scorpion* ended up firing at both these two British ships.

When the last gun on the *Lawrence* was knocked out of action and 80% of the crew was dead or wounded, Perry boarded the ship's (amazingly only slightly damaged) skiff and had himself rowed back to the undamaged *Niagara*. The *Lawrence*, helpless, hauled down its flag.

Perry immediately dispatched Elliot to take the skiff and row back to urge the four small ships at the end of the American battle line (the schooners *Porcupine*, *Somers*, *Trippe* and *Tigress*) to come up into the battle. Perry himself had the *Niagara* head into the British line where the *Detroit* and the *Queen Charlotte* (both now battered and with heavy casualties, including all the senior officers) were struggling to regroup.

By this point in the battle, the riggings on both main British ships were smashed to the point that the ships were virtually unmaneuverable. This factor combined with having only inexperienced junior officers left standing at the helms apparently resulted in the bowsprits of the two British ships to become entangled. They drifted locked together as the few remaining crewmen tried to clear the tangle.

When the unscathed *Niagara* came up, it could sail around the two ships, battering them with broadside after broadside from its huge 32-pounder carronades. To quote Colonel Theodore Roosevelt in his history of the War of 1812: *the Niagara stood down and broke the British line, firing her port battery into the Chippewa, Little Belt and Lady Provost and her starboard battery into the Detroit, Queen Charlotte and Hunter, raking on both sides.* The British were forced to strike their colors.

Immediately after the victory, everyone, including Elliot, was hailed as a hero. The country, after two years of military bad news, urgently needed a victory and some heroes. It was only later that questions were raised about Elliot's actions. A Board of Inquiry, despite wide differences in testimony, including transcripts of the testimony at Commander Barclay's court martial, exonerated Elliot (some say more for public relations than objective judgment). Elliot and Perry were enemies for the balance of their lives. Claiming that Perry was slandering him about his actions, he challenged Perry to a duel. Perry declined.

The above version of events was the traditional story that came down through history. Perry was apparently much better "connected" than Elliot politically, and he got the most favorable publicity. There was even some talk of grooming Perry to run for President at some point in the future.

In all fairness to Elliot, there are some prominent historians, like David Frew, who feel that Elliot may have been unjustly maligned. They have reconstructed, from a number of other sources, in both the U.S. and England, a somewhat different scenario. For those who want to explore this controversy in depth, it would be important to look into Elliot's side of the affair.

Appendix I - The Courtesy of Warfare of the Period

Under "Luck" the instance of the Lady from Amherstburg and the dinner at Fort George were discussed. There were other instances of this sort of conduct. The British officers killed in the Battle of Lake Erie were all buried with full military honors. Perry put Barclay up in a luxurious (by frontier standards) apartment in Erie while he was recovering from his wounds.

After the end of the war, Chauncey invited Yeo and his officers to visit Sackett's Harbor and then arranged transportation for them from there to New York to take ship back to England. (Otherwise Yeo and his staff would have had to wait until the ice cleared on the St. Lawrence and then sail out past Newfoundland and across the stormy North Atlantic in winter).

With few exceptions, like the "Christmas Truce" in the WW I trenches and the formal but polite reception extended to the first American troops landing in Japan after the surrender it seems like War of 1812 type courteous acts have disappeared from modern warfare.

Appendix J - The Ojibwa Legacy

The Ojibwa Tribe, the allies of the British who tried to prevent the American landings at the Battle of York, is remembered today for a quite different reason. In 1922, a Canadian nurse, Rene Caisse, learned from a Medicine Man of that tribe about an herbal medicine that turned out to be a form of immune system stimulant with some reported success in fighting cancer. Although the medical profession is still somewhat divided about its efficacy (for instance, Dr. Brusch, President Kennedy's personal physician, was a major supporter of the research), it is sold today at health food stores throughout the US and Canada under names like "Ojibwa Compound" and "Essiac" (Caisse spelled backwards).

Appendix K. Potential "Three Strikes" in Some Other American Wars from the Revolution through World War II

1. The Three Strikes of the American Revolution

Although not as dramatic and clear cut a correlation, there were a series of three interrelated victories in the same period in time and geographic region during the American Revolution that might be viewed as the crucial "Three Strikes" that convinced England to agree to end the conflict. These victories were:

a) King's Mountain, October 1780

The virtual annihilation of the loyalist militia on the South Carolina frontier forced the British to revise their southern strategy. This battle demonstrated that the loyalist militia, particularly in a large pitched battle could not begin to make up for a shortage of regulars. Without more reliable and substantial Loyalist militia, the British forces of Redcoats in the south found themselves overextended and vulnerable. For the southern strategy to succeed, it was going to be necessary to move down a large number of regular troops from the northern colonies or England.

b) Cowpens, January 1781

This sudden unexpected defeat of a substantial Redcoat force by American regulars stopped the British offensive momentum in the south and renewed the spirits of American forces. At this engagement, the British were unpleasantly surprised by the professionalism of the new Continental Army. The Americans, on the other hand, were encouraged to initiate the final offensive campaign that ultimately brought the war to an end.

c) Yorktown, October 1781

This was not really a pitched battle but rather a protracted siege that ended in the surrender of a substantial British army. At the end of the long campaign which began at Cowpens, Cornwallis' army had retreated to Yorktown to await the supplies and reinforcements requested from General Clinton in New York.

Unknown to Cornwallis, Admiral De Grasse had temporarily slipped away from his station guarding French interests in the Caribbean and brought his fleet of forty warships north. The ships brought with them a substantial contingent of French regulars and, equally important, French large siege cannon.

The British had not anticipated the timely arrival of a major French fleet and Clinton felt he did not have the naval forces available to break through the French blockade. He was therefore prevented from reinforcing, resupplying or evacuating Cornwallis' army by sea. In addition to the blockade, Cornwallis had also not expected the large contingent of French regulars along with their siege artillery that had been landed by the French fleet to fight alongside Washington's Continentals.

Surrounded, outnumbered, his back to the French controlled sea and running out of supplies Cornwallis surrendered. It was difficult enough for Cornwallis' Redcoats to march out to surrender to this army of their upstart colonists but the real ignominy was to have to march out past row on row of the despised French regulars in their white uniforms. This operation was both the zenith of French-American cooperation in the war and the end of major British military operations in America.

d) The Possible Flaw in the Categorizing

In retrospect, this example, unfortunately, possibly may not be listed as a true "Three Strike" example. That is because of a *deus ex machine* aspect, the timely arrival of the French fleet, troops and cannon. Without this factor, Clinton may have been able to send the ships, supplies and reinforcements needed to extricate Cornwallis for his dilemma. However, if it can be shown that the American successes at Kings Mountain and Cowpens were the factors that actually convinced the French to intervene militarily at Yorktown, the Three Strikes category might still apply.

2. The Three Strikes of WWII

Almost at the other end of the time spectrum were the Three Strikes of WWII.

a) Coral Sea May 4-8 1942

Only five months after Pearl Harbor the first of three interrelated battles was fought. This first one was triggered by the need to turn back the Japanese invasion fleet headed for New Guinea. It is noted in history for being the first major naval battle where the ships engaged never actually saw one another. The real interest in this battle should be that, in it, the Japanese lost the availability of two fleet carriers and one light carrier. The light carrier Shōhō was sunk, the fleet carrier Shōkak was so heavily damaged that it had to be sent to back dry dock for major repairs and the fleet carrier Zuikaku had lost so many planes and pilots that it had to go back to Kure to be re-staffed and re-equipped. As a result, these carriers were not available for the major Japanese attack on Midway the following month.

On the American side, the carrier Yorktown was heavily damaged but did make it back to Pearl Harbor and its damaged, but luckily still functioning, shipyard. (Coincidentally, as listed above, the Battle of Yorktown was one of the potential "Three Strikes" of the American Revolution).

b) Midway June 3-7 1942

With the losses (see above) at the Battle of the Coral Sea, the Japanese could only deploy four (of the six in the Pearl Harbor attack) fleet aircraft carriers for the assault on Midway atoll. The American carrier fleet included the Enterprise, the Hornet and the (hastily repaired) Yorktown. In addition, the US had the "fixed aircraft carrier "of Midway Island airfield available.

The Battle was fiercely fought with heavy losses of planes, pilots and ships on both sides but, in the end, the US Navy prevailed. All four Japanese carriers were sunk and three hundred of their planes and pilots lost. The US Navy lost the Yorktown but its crew was mostly saved. If the Japanese had had the availability of the two fleet carriers and one light carrier that were lost to them because of the earlier Battle of the Coral Sea, the Battle of Midway conceivably could have gone the other way.

Midway is considered by many as the "high tide of the Japanese Naval Forces". After Midway the Japanese Navy was largely on the defensive and retreating for the balance of the war.

c) Battle of Milne Bay (and the Kokoda Track)

Many Americans have never heard of this battle. This is to some degree because it was largely an action of our Australian allies. The US forces involved were primarily engineers and pilots. There were, few, if any, American combat troops.When the American code breakers learned that the Japanese were planning to build an airbase at Milne Bay on the extreme southeastern tip of New

Guinea to support their planned invasion of Australia, General McArthur decided to preempt them. He dispatched Australian troops and American engineering battalions who landed and built an airfield at that same location under extreme climate and disease conditions. By August that year there were 9,000 men at the base, primarily Australian troops. Two squadrons of the RAAF were already on site.

Believing the base was only lightly defended, the Japanese sent an invasion fleet to seize the base. This base was vital to Japan's plan for the invasion of Australia. From this base they intended to provide the air cover for the major land attack they were planning on launching across New Guinea, on the Kokoda Track, to secure a base for the planned invasion.

Although the RAAF fighters succeeded in damaging and destroying many of the landing barges on the way to Milne, the Japanese did succeed in landing thousands of marines. Thanks to their carrier losses in the earlier Battles of the Coral Sea and Midway, this Japanese landing and attack had no air cover. Relentless bombing and strafing attacks by the RAAF and American aircraft plus the numerical and firepower advantage of the Australian and American defenders drove the Japanese back to the landing beaches where the survivors were evacuated by their navy.

Without the air cover they had counted on being able to receive from the planned Japanese air base at Milne (that never was built) the plan for the major Japanese land assault across the New Guineas' Kokoda Track had to be abandoned. Only much later was it recognized that this relatively small battle was actually the "high tide of the Japanese land forces". From this point on, the Japanese land forces were also on the defensive and in retreat for the rest of the war. The invasion of Australia was thwarted.

Bibliography

Benn, Carl, *Guide to the War of 1812,* Osprey Publishing 2002

Borneman, Walter, *1812, The War that Forged a Nation,* Harper/Collins 2004

Daugham, George, *1812, The Navy's War,* Basic Books 2011

Frew, David, *Perry's Lake Erie Fleet,* History Press 2012

Hitsman, J. Mackay (updated by Graves, Donald), *The Incredible War of 1812,* Robin Brass Studio 1999

Hickey, Donald, *The War of 1812,* Univ. of Illinois Pub. 2012

Laxer, James, *Tecumseh & Brock,* House of Anani Press 2012

Lardas, Mark, *Great Lakes Warships 1812-1815,* Osprey Publishing 2012

Roosevelt, Theodore, *The Naval War of 1812*, G. P. Putnam 1882

Rybka, Walter, *The Lake Erie Campaign of 1813,* History Press 2012

Skaggs, David & Altoff, Gerald, *A Signal Victory.* Naval Institute Press 1997

Symonds, Craig, *Decision at Sea,* Oxford Univ. Press 2001

Taylor, Allen, *The Civil War of 1812,* Vintage Books (Random House) 2010

Thomas, Richard, *The Essiac Report,* Alternative Treatment Information Network 1993

War of 1812 Magazine

Many subjects were looked up on *Wikipedia*

Newspaper-Boston Weekly Messenger Oct.1, 1813, May 13, 1814

ABOUT THE AUTHOR

William (Bill) Miller was born in Brooklyn and received his BS and MS from MIT. His fifty years of business experience involved thirty-two years in management, including five as Chief Technology Officer of Welch Allyn, twelve as Vice President of Research and Development, plus five as a Division General Manager, of American Sterilizer. Prior to that, he had held a succession of management positions at General Electric. He served in the U.S. Air Force during the Korean War. A retired Licensed Professional Engineer, he was active in technology during his entire life and holds twenty patents. His previous publications include one business book, five magazine articles, two economic development studies, one hymn, and numerous booklets.

During his career life, and particularly since retirement, he has been very active with charities, church groups and other non-profits. He just retired from the Board of Erie Meals on Wheels after many years as Treasurer. A lifelong supporter of MIT, William served as Regional Chairman, Educational Counselor and as Secretary of his class. His current work as a Guide for the Erie Maritime Museum is the motivator for this book.

Bill is listed in a number of *Who's Who* publications, including *Who's Who in the East* and *Who's Who in Science and Technology*.

www.ingramcontent.com/pod-product-compliance
Lightning Source LLC
Chambersburg PA
CBHW060401090426
42734CB00011B/2215